£2·10

THE CAMBRIDGE ECONOMIC HANDBOOKS

General Editors:

J. M. KEYNES (Lord Keynes)	**1922–1936**
D. H. ROBERTSON (Sir Dennis Robertson)	**1936–1946**
C. W. GUILLEBAUD	**1946–1956**
C. W. GUILLEBAUD ⎫ MILTON FRIEDMAN ⎭	**1956–**

POPULATION

IAN BOWEN

Formerly Fellow of All Souls College, Oxford

DIGSWELL PLACE
JAMES NISBET & CO. LTD.
CAMBRIDGE
AT THE UNIVERSITY PRESS

The first Cambridge Economic Handbook on
POPULATION was written by Harold Wright
and published in 1923

First Published 1954

Reprinted . . . 1955
Reprinted . . . 1960
Reprinted . . . 1964
Reprinted . . . 1966

James Nisbet and Company Limited
Digswell Place, Welwyn, Herts
and the Cambridge University Press
in Association with the University of Chicago Press

INTRODUCTION

Soon after the war of 1914–18 there seemed to be a place for a series of short introductory handbooks, "intended to convey to the ordinary reader and to the uninitiated student some conception of the general principles of thought which economists now apply to economic problems."

This Series was planned and edited by the late Lord Keynes under the title "Cambridge Economic Handbooks" and he wrote for it a General Editorial Introduction of which the words quoted above formed part. In 1936 Keynes handed over the editorship of the Series to Mr. D. H. Robertson, who held it till 1946, when he was succeeded by Mr. C. W. Guillebaud.

It was symptomatic of the changes which had been taking place in the inter-war period in the development of economics, changes associated in a considerable measure with the work and influence of Keynes himself, that within a few years the text of part of the Editorial Introduction should have needed revision. In its original version the last paragraph of the Introduction ran as follows:

"Even on matters of principle there is not yet a complete unanimity of opinion amongst professional economists. Generally speaking, the writers of these volumes believe themselves to be orthodox members of the Cambridge School of Economics. At any rate, most of their ideas about the subject, and even their prejudices, are traceable to the contact they have enjoyed with the writings and lectures of the two economists who have chiefly influenced Cambridge thought for the past fifty years, Dr. Marshall and Professor Pigou."

Keynes later amended this concluding paragraph to read:

"Even on matters of principle there is not yet a complete unanimity of opinion amongst professional students of the subject. Immediately after the war (of 1914–18) daily economic events were of such a startling character as to divert attention from theoretical complexities. But today, economic science has recovered its wind. Traditional treatments and traditional solutions are being questioned, improved and revised. In the end this activity of research should clear up controversy. But for the moment controversy and doubt are increased. The writers of this Series must apologize to the general reader and to the beginner if many parts of their subject have not yet reached to a degree of certainty and lucidity which would make them easy and straightforward reading."

Many though by no means all the controversies which Keynes had in mind when he penned these words have since been resolved. The new ideas and new criticisms, which then seemed to threaten to overturn the old orthodoxy, have, in the outcome, been absorbed within it and have served rather to strengthen and deepen it, by adding needed modifications and changing emphasis, and by introducing an altered and on the whole more precise terminology. The undergrowth which for a time concealed that main stream of economic thought to which Keynes referred in his initial comment and to which he contributed so greatly has by now been largely cleared away so that there is again a large measure of agreement among economists of all countries on the fundamental theoretical aspects of their subject.

This agreement on economic analysis is accompanied by wide divergence of views on questions of economic policy. These reflect both different estimates of the quantitative importance of one or another of the conflicting forces involved in any prediction about the consequences of a policy measure and different value judgments about the desirability of the predicted outcome. It still remains as true today as it was when

Keynes wrote that—to quote once more from his Introduction:

"The Theory of Economics does not furnish a body of settled conclusions immediately applicable to policy. It is a method rather than a doctrine, an apparatus of the mind, a technique of thinking, which helps its possessor to draw correct conclusions."

This method, while in one sense eternally the same, is in another ever changing. It is continually being applied to new problems raised by the continual shifts in policy views. This is reflected in the wide range of topics covered by the Cambridge Economic Handbooks already published, and in the continual emergence of new topics demanding coverage. Such a series as this should accordingly itself be a living entity, growing and adapting to the changing interests of the times, rather than a fixed number of essays on a set plan.

The wide welcome given to the Series has amply justified the judgment of its founder. Apart from its circulation in the British Empire, it has been published from the start in the United States of America, and translations of the principal volumes have appeared in a number of foreign languages.

The present change to joint Anglo-American editorship is designed to increase still further the usefulness of the Series by expanding the range of potential topics, authors and readers alike. It will succeed in its aim if it enables us to bring to a wide audience on both sides of the Atlantic lucid explanations and significant applications of "that technique of thinking" which is the hallmark of economics as a science.

C. W. GUILLEBAUD

April 1957   MILTON FRIEDMAN

PREFACE

The connection between economic development and population change is not simple, nor necessarily constant over the years. The classical economists bravely undertook to define the connection; when their generalizations had been exposed by events as over-simplifications, economists began to drop the discussion altogether, or merely to re-state the older doctrines. Nevertheless, a connection probably exists, and this short study attempts to outline how the student of economics, or the general reader, might now approach the problem. References in the text have been kept as brief as possible. Full references are given at the end in the select bibliography, which may serve as a guide to further reading.

I am much indebted to my friends and critics at Hull, who have helped in the planning and production of this book, especially to Miss Joyce Bellamy, Mr. George Maxcy, Mr. Leslie Smyth, Mr. Martyn Webb and to my wife; and for the secretarial assistance provided by Miss Olive Bevan and Miss Barbara Wood.

IAN BOWEN

HULL, 1954

CONTENTS

INTRODUCTION TO THE SERIES v

PREFACE ix

PART I—INTRODUCTORY SURVEY

CHAPTER I

POPULATION AND ECONOMICS

§ 1. THE ECONOMIC CRITERION 3

§ 2. CLASSIFICATION OF FACTORS AFFECTING POPULATION
CHANGE 8

§ 3. OUTLINE OF TREATMENT TO BE FOLLOWED . . 13

CHAPTER II

WORLD POPULATION

§ 1. POPULATION ESTIMATES AND EXTRAPOLATION OF
TRENDS 15

§ 2. VITAL RATES FOR DIFFERENT REGIONS . . . 22

§ 3. REPRODUCTION RATES 25

§ 4. LOGISTIC CURVES AND THEIR LIMITATIONS . . 28

§ 5. POPULATION PROJECTIONS OF THE 1940's . . 29

§ 6. DIFFERING PERCENTAGE RATES OF INCREASE . 37

§ 7. WORLD POPULATION AND FOOD SUPPLIES . . 40

§ 8. POPULATION AND RAW MATERIALS . . . 50

CHAPTER III

BRITAIN'S POPULATION

§ 1. ESTIMATES AND TRENDS **54**

§ 2. URBANIZATION **63**

§ 3. AGE AND SEX DISTRIBUTION .   .   . **66**

§ 4. DISTRIBUTION BY OCCUPATIONS .   .   . **70**

PART II—ANALYSIS

CHAPTER IV

THE MALTHUSIAN THEORY

§ 1. MALTHUS AS A PUBLICIST **81**

§ 2. MALTHUS'S POSTULATES AND ARGUMENTS . **88**

§ 3. PECULIARITIES OF THE MALTHUSIAN DOCTRINE . **95**

§ 4. THE "QUALIFIED" MALTHUSIAN DOCTRINE . **104**

§ 5. NEO-MALTHUSIANISM **111**

§ 6. EQUALITY OF POPULATION WITH FOOD .   . **119**

§ 7. NEO-GODWINIANISM **121**

CHAPTER V

THEORIES OF STATIC EQUILIBRIUM

§ 1. THE IDEA OF A MAXIMUM POPULATION .   .   . **124**

§ 2. THE IDEA OF A MINIMUM POPULATION .   .   . **128**

§ 3. THE OPTIMUM POPULATION ON STATIC ASSUMPTIONS **130**

§ 4. ECOLOGICAL EQUILIBRIUM **134**

§ 5. THE MALTHUSIAN AND GODWINIAN RESULTS . **140**

CHAPTER VI

EQUILIBRIUM AND WORKING POPULATION

§ 1. THE ECONOMIC DEMAND FOR LABOUR . . . 142
§ 2. THE SUPPLY OF LABOUR 144
§ 3. THE BALANCE OF DEMAND AND SUPPLY . . 149

CHAPTER VII

THE EXPANDING ECONOMY

§ 1. CAPITAL PER HEAD OF POPULATION . . . 155
§ 2. ECONOMIC GROWTH 159

CHAPTER VIII

INTERNATIONAL MIGRATION

§ 1. TYPES OF MIGRATION 167
§ 2. LONG-TERM, PERMANENT INTERNATIONAL MIGRATION 169
§ 3. SHORT-TERM INTERNATIONAL MIGRATION . . 185
§ 4. MIGRATION AND TRADE CYCLES 187

PART III—FUTURE PROSPECTS

CHAPTER IX

GREAT BRITAIN

§ 1. DEMOGRAPHIC, ECONOMIC, POLITICAL AND SOCIAL
  OBJECTIVES AND FACTORS 199
§ 2. ECONOMIC ARGUMENTS FOR A STABLE OR FALLING
  POPULATION 203

§ 3. THE SUPPLY OF RAW MATERIALS 205
§ 4. THE BALANCE OF PAYMENTS ARGUMENT . . 208
§ 5. COUNTER-ARGUMENTS (DEMOGRAPHIC AND ECONOMIC)
      IN FAVOUR OF A STABLE OR INCREASING POPULATION 211
§ 6. POLITICAL AND SOCIAL PROS AND CONS . . 219

CHAPTER X

WORLD POPULATION

§ 1. THE FOOD PROBLEM 227
§ 2. ECONOMIC PROSPECTS 234
§ 3. SOCIAL CHANGES 245
     BIBLIOGRAPHY 249

POPULATION

PART I

INTRODUCTORY SURVEY

CHAPTER I

POPULATION AND ECONOMICS

§ 1. *The Economic Criterion.* The question how many people there ought to be in any country can be answered in many ways, according to the values to which the answer has reference. In this study, the size, and the rate of growth, of the British (and Northern Irish) population in relation to its economic welfare, even though this concept is itself inexact and difficult to define, are the chief subjects to be discussed. But the British population is especially vulnerable to changes in world economic conditions, and these conditions are in turn linked inexorably with world population changes.

The difficulty of defining a value criterion for the subject arises in an acute form, since what has to be discussed is not merely one population but at least two (the British and the rest of the world)—and many more according as other countries and continents have to be considered as separate problems. If values are consciously sought the discussion may become excessively philosophical, while ignoring the issue may lead to the unintentional adoption of unnecessarily biased assumptions. What size and rate of growth ought the British population to have over the next fifty years? Is it to be 2 per cent or 4 per cent of world population—fifty or a hundred or twenty-five millions? Any of these sizes might be consistent with preserving life and conserving *some* British influence on the civilized life of the world. Some additional criterion is required by which to test these alternatives.

3

Professor F. W. Notestein, in reviewing[1] the (British) Report of the Royal Commission on Population,[2] remarks on the "in part almost mystical, but universal and probably healthy, reluctance to see one's own group dwindle in size". He goes on to maintain that the Commission's arguments on the question of British emigration to the Dominions were "based more on sentiment than on a rational calculation of national or commercial advantage". Yet even Professor Notestein himself is here introducing unconscious assumptions, his underlying notion seeming to be that "commercial advantage" is "rational", while "sentiment" is "irrational", a value judgment that is itself open to dispute. The immediate object of any state may be material wealth, but it would be a special and peculiar society wherein material wealth was the sole objective; historically most societies have pursued other ends as well, with material wealth regarded as a means to attaining those ends, or to their fuller realization, and it is a fallacy to suppose that men need television sets in order to receive only advertisements for better or different television sets. The sounder line of criticism of nationalistic bias in population theories is that it conflicts with values which may be more defensible.

The way in which the Royal Commission itself tackled the problem deserves some attention. The Commission began its report by sketching the history of world population since 1750, and of British population in relation to it. The Report remarks [3] that "Great Britain's share in the population of the continent [of Europe] rose from 5·7 per cent in 1801 to 9 per cent in 1900 . . . if her population had not been growing, and growing rapidly, her

[1] *Population Studies*, Vol. III, No. 3, p. 237, and cf. Hubback, 1947, p. 116.
[2] Cmd. 7695, published by H.M.S.O., June 1949.
[3] Cmd. 7695, 1949, par. 21, p. 8.

leadership could not have endured more than a few years"
—hence, it is argued, the *economic* development of the
world (including that of Britain itself) would have been
lower in 1949 than it then was. Furthermore—and at
this point the Report's "political" values become more
explicit—"the influence of Britain and of British ideas
would be far less extensive than it is to-day". As a
perhaps rather unexpected example of this influence the
Report refers to "the expansion of the United States as
an English-speaking nation" which was "greatly encouraged by the large emigration of Britons" in the
nineteenth century.

This approach, like Professor Notestein's, is of considerable interest because of its implications.   To the authors
of the Report "British ideas" is a term that includes
"American ideas", in 1949, a date at which the distinction
between them was often considered to be significant.
How much weight indeed ought to be given to such concepts as "British ideas" or "the American way of life"?
It may be natural that groups should wish to see ideologies,
to which their own group-name is attached, flourish and
expand their influence.   But experience has shown
patriotic fervour to be a misleading and destructive force,
as well as, at times, a noble and preserving one.   What
do we understand, in any case, by "British ideas"?
Whatever these are now, they were different in 1950 from
what they were in 1900, and the population movements
under consideration span the centuries.   Or is all this
talk of "British ideas" (or French or American ideas) a
mere rationalization, as Professor Notestein has hinted,
of a primitive urge for group survival, and for national
self-preservation?   Primitive urges are not necessarily
to be condemned; without them there would be no
problems of population, and perhaps no population.   But

in this instance they might be rationalized by each nation in such a way as to legislate for perpetual warfare, for if the members of each separate population, or a sufficient number of them, consider that it has a sacred mission to expand (invoking the law of the ultimate survival of the fittest, and deeming their own special characteristics to be relatively the best) then international anarchy and strife are inevitable; for the power to expand numbers is very considerable.

Fear of this impasse has toned down the explicit recommendations of most populationists, populationists being defined as those who maintain that some degree (usually a high one) of continuing net natural increase in the numbers of their own nation is a desirable objective. Because of it they have taken refuge in rather vague reference to "ideas", "ways of life" and so on, rather than advocate primitive group expansion. Their argument has then run somewhat as follows. Certain ideas are good; these ideas have been preserved and developed best by certain national groups (for instance the French), and have been best expressed in the French language; therefore it is good for these ideas, this civilized mode of life, to spread. But, of course, the rational objector may here interpose, these ideas might be spread by education and not by birth. At this point the populationist appeals to history; without demographic forces to maintain it, he will argue, a civilized mode will decline and perish—this we know inductively from endless instances. For example, M. Marcel Reinhard writes of the French Canadians [1]:

"Un peuple est né, il a sauvegardé ses traditions et ses croyances. Ce triomphe est du à sa vitalité, frap-

[1] Reinhard [1949], p. 389.

pante illustration du rôle de la démographie ou, plus
exactement, de la natalité . . . Les Canadiens français
forment, en effet, environ le tiers de la population du
Dominion: 3·4 millions sur 12·5 . . . En 1763 ils
n'étaient guère que 65,000, mais déjà remarquablement
prolifiques.''

And in similar terms the same authority deplores the
decline of the French birth-rate in France, and the in-
effectiveness of the legislation designed to arrest it and to
ameliorate social conditions.

Populationism in its extreme form has always been
repugnant to humanitarian critics, because of the false
values on which it has seemed to rest. It has always
seemed to be based on blind, and ultimately mutually
destructive, group loyalties. Fascists have been notable
populationists, and so have militarists of every persuasion.
So too have been, and are, the more obscurantist religions
of the world, those that rely on faith rather than on
reason or on the wider forms of education. Considerations of agricultural space or raw material supplies or
social hygiene will not deter them, perhaps because there
are always many of these supplies in the possession of
unbelievers.

But the existence of these extreme views should not be
allowed wholly to discredit the notion that births may
be too low in some societies for the realization of a good
end. That end, for the purposes of this book, must be
defined as broadly as possible, and from the point of
view of the world as a whole. It will be assumed that it
is right to think of the world community as a single large
group; it will be assumed that this group is composed
of individuals who want (or would want if sufficiently en-
lightened) economic sufficiency, security and advancement,

as a means to exercising their physical and intellectual powers for improvement of mankind's quality of life. These assumptions are not necessarily realistic—it may not even be true that the majority of men are yet capable of regarding themselves as citizens of one world; but the assumption is nevertheless made.

It is not suggested that national and religious differences will not continue, nor that they will cease to be important. One difficulty in the formula just proposed is that there can be no general agreement on what is meant by "improving" the quality of life, and members of some groups will interpret this as attainable only in terms of the extension of their own beliefs or practices. But an assumption on values has to be made, and the one made here is that such differences of view will be, in principle, less important than the common agreement (open or tacit) of many individuals that there are some common values for the world community as a whole. This is not a treatise on political science, so the means of expressing popular will on these values need not here be discussed.

Evidently this assumption still does not provide an exact measure against which to compare possible different population rates of growth. There may be, by this test— which is necessarily rough—more than one "right size" or "best rate of change" for the British and for the world populations. But the subject can be rescued from vagueness by the fact that not all paths of advance are open to the world, or to the national economy. The range of choice is severely restricted.

§ 2. *Classification of Factors affecting Population Change.* The economic criterion discussed above was defined in terms of (economic) "sufficiency, security and advancement", and the ideas that these terms represent perhaps need to be explained a little further. All three words have meaning only in relation to existing conditions, and to various individuals' points of view; what is "sufficiency" to a British civil servant might be gross poverty to an American business man, and what a Belgian coal-miner regarded as "security" a British docker might take to be uncertainty of employment. But though the terms are necessarily relative, each of them indicates unambiguously a direction in which the economic system may, or may not, move.

There is an approximate, though not complete, correspondence between the three objectives and the customary division of time adopted by economists. Very roughly economic "sufficiency" (which might also be called the "optimum level[1] of real income per head") is an objective to be realized in the short or medium term; economic advancement is a long-term concept; while economic security for the most part (though not exclusively) means avoidance of the hazards of periodic, or cyclical, fluctuations in employment.

Whether or not a particular size of population satisfies the economic criterion depends upon the point of view. The definition of an "optimum" population is therefore a matter of some difficulty, and the question is discussed at much greater length in chapter five.

It is part of our task to examine not only what size and composition a population should have, to meet some criterion, but also how it came to be what it is. The factors which determine the size and the rate of growth of the population of any particular place, whether of the world or of some political unit, are almost certainly very numerous. Fortunately, it may be reasonable to classify

[1], I.e., the highest income that is attainable without a more than proportionate violation of some other criterion which can be valued.

them at the outset, and so to introduce an order into our thinking, without however prejudging which of the factors, or groups of factors, are most important.

The factors which affect population growth may, like the economic criterion, be divided broadly into three: long-term, short-term and cyclical. Into the first of these classes must come such influences as a slow change in the size of families such as follows, for instance, the spread of knowledge of contraception; into the second come sudden migratory flows due to war or natural disaster; into the third, those rises and falls in the birth-rate or in the migration rates that have been demonstrated, in some instances, to occur in times of boom and slump. The reader will no doubt have observed that these three examples are each of a different *character*, however, not only in respect of time-scale but because *family size* is largely demographically determined, *war* is mainly political in origin, and *booms and slumps* are economic phenomena.

The factors have been schematically represented below, and are divided horizontally into three rows representing Demographic, Economic and Political factors, these in turn being divided according to whether they are affecting population growth in the Long-term (decades or centuries), the Short-term (single years or less) or Cyclical (more or less regular intervals of a few years). Thus as a first approximation it may be useful to think of nine main types cf factor that determine the size, or rate of growth, of population. Let p summarize the combined effects of nine separate factors, a to k. These factors are not necessarily independent of each other through time.

This representation is merely schematic; the letter shown in each "box" represents one type of factor at work on one time-scale. For example, a slow but steady

Table I

	Long Term	Short Term	Cyclical	Total Category Effects
Demographic . .	*a*	*b*	*c*	*d*
Economic . .	*e*	*f*	*g*	*h*
Political . . .	*i*	*j*	*k*	*l*
Total time effects .	*m*	*n*	*o*	*p*

decline in the intention to have large families would be classified under *a*, as a long-term demographic factor. A steady trend downwards (unfavourably) in the terms of trade of a country would be listed under *e*, as a long-term economic consideration (in this case inimical to population growth). The election, for a short period of office, of a government with an exceptionally generous family allowance scheme in its party platform would be counted as a *j* factor, and so on.

All this may seem obvious, and the mere systematization of a truism. But there are three reasons for introducing the scheme at this stage of the argument. First, this truism is one that is often mentioned verbally, especially at the beginning of treatises, and then in fact ignored. The demographic specialist mentions the importance of economic and political factors, but tends to regard them as ripples on the slow, steady tide of the demographic swell. The political theorist (or historian) sometimes ignores the demographic and economic cross-currents. Even the economist is not always wholly immune from the specialist's arrogance. The present study, partly because it is by an economist, will stress the importance of economic factors; but this is not the only reason for stressing that—the other reason is that in many discussions of population problems the economic factors have tended to be grossly under-emphasized.

Secondly, the scheme will serve to remind us not to fall into the opposite, and equally egregious error, of concentrating attention on economic factors to the *exclusion* of the weighing up of more or less independent demographic and political factors, which at certain points of history have the greatest importance for population growth.

Since the factors represented by the different letters are not necessarily independent, a short-term "political" event, say a war of short duration, with heavy casualties, may not only affect population directly but may also affect some other factor, for instance b (by creating a surplus of females over males and a lower marriage rate), or even c, since the aftermath of the war may be an exceptionally high birth-rate for a few years, which will tend to cause every twenty-five to thirty years thereafter a cyclical bump in the average birth-rate.

Any one of the classified factors may have an effect on any other, and hence eventually a feed back effect on itself. The problem of determining how population growth has occurred is the problem of writing down correctly all these functional relationships. In practice this is well beyond our present powers of analysis. The most that can be hoped for is that the chief functional relationships can be picked out, and perhaps the second order, or even third order, effects in certain instances.

To discover the functional relationships for any particular period would not necessarily mean (even if it were feasible) establishing their value for all time. In some circumstances an economic factor, say a lowering in the standard of life, may have a quite different direct effect on population growth than in others; sometimes an economic change will provoke a major political change, and at others be quite neutral in its political effects; sometimes demographic changes have immediate economic results, and sometimes their results work out only over several decades.

The scheme may be given whatever degree of precision is required. The terms Demographic, Economic and Political may be defined as we choose, so long as they provide an exhaustive basis for classifying the factors that affect population change. Demographic factors are intended to include all matters relating to size of families to physical health of individuals and communities, and to changes in the structure or functioning of the human organism; economic factors are those which arise from the organization of human beings as producers and consumers, and from the scarcity of raw materials to satisfy their needs; and political factors cover all residual items, such as the influences of the forms of society and of government, of the pursuit of power, and of the institutions which owe their origin to habit or imagination.

§ 3. *Outline of Treatment to be Followed.*   The first part of this book is intended as a survey rather than as an analysis, as will be seen from the chapter headings. Nevertheless, it may be useful to look all the time for scraps of evidence which bear both (*a*) on the criterion of judging "success" (i.e., whether a population is of the right size), and (*b*) on the factors which have made population what it is. In Part II, the analysis of population growth is first considered historically (including the explanations of Malthus and others); then the economic criterion of "success" is discussed in detail (Chapter V); and in Chapter VI the same ideas are broadened to cover rates of growth as well as size.   Finally, international migration is both surveyed and analysed in relation to the preceding discussion.

In Part III the future prospects of Britain and the World are surveyed.

Before turning to later chapters, the reader might find it useful to try to classify into one box or another of Table I the factors which, in his experience, seem principally to have affected changes in the population of his own neighbourhood, county and country, or of other divisions well known to him.   It is likely to become apparent to him that many factors other than " demographic " seem prima facie to have been operative.   (In this chapter the word " demographic " has been applied in a somewhat loose sense, though one justified by usage ; " demological " would perhaps be a more accurate substitute.)

CHAPTER II

WORLD POPULATION

§ 1. *Population Estimates and Extrapolation of Trends.* It is evidently necessary to know how many people there are in the world, where they live and their likely rate of increase in the future, in order to discuss population problems at all satisfactorily, and some fairly well established estimates and forecasts are fortunately available. But estimates and forecasts are by their nature uncertain, and their credibility and hence the validity of using them require careful assessment.

Anyone who has filled up a census return knows that some slight inaccuracy may quite easily be recorded on it; even conscientious citizens may fall into unintentional error, and not all citizens are conscientious; some are not literate. In some countries a majority of adults may well be indifferent or even hostile to enumeration, nor are enumerators immune from fallibility and inexactitude. Despite these expected shortcomings census returns are regarded as, at present, giving the best count of human beings that can be obtained, and as being, for the practical purpose of discussions of broad issues, sufficiently exact.

But not all "countries" (that is, separate political units) have even a census.[1] For those with no censuses, estimates have to be made on the basis of such non-censal statistics as seem to be relevant. Hence the recorded total of world population in 1950, for example, contains

[1] For instance the Belgian Congo, Morocco, Mauritius and the British Cameroons, to pick out a few. The "type of estimate" column of Table I of the United Nations' Demographic Yearbook for 1949–50 gives some details of the basis of the estimates in a convenient form.

a considerable margin of error.   The error is much greater for Africa, Asia and South America than for Western Europe and North America.

The possible error in the totals increases for earlier dates.   The estimates even of European population in the seventeenth and eighteenth centuries are notoriously insecure.   The figures for Asia, Africa and South America in 1900 have also been hotly debated, and frequently revised.[1]   The technical details of these disputes need not be described, but the possibility of error must be mentioned since it limits the effectiveness of arguments based upon the trends in the estimates.

To look to the future, population figures must be extrapolated, which means writing down figures in a sequence justified by the rate of changes in rate, observed in a past sequence.   Evidently this justification may assume that the past rate (or change of rate) will persist.   By varying the assumptions (that is by choosing different rates as the "key" rates) different extrapolations, or guesses, as to future population can be made.   But if the assumption is that the governing rate will be very different in the future from past and current rates then arguments have to be adduced to support the likelihood of the change assumed.   The past history of population includes instances of very important and large changes in birth-rates, death-rates and other vital statistics directly affecting the change in total population.   It is a matter of judgment whether to predict any further large change in human habits affecting births and deaths.

Most extrapolations, or guesses, about the future size of population are based on assumptions not of substantial

[1] For example, a World Health Organization publication (see Swaroop 1951) gave an estimate of the population of Africa in 1900 as 141 million, whereas a publication of the U.N. Department of Social Affairs (Population Division) gave an estimate of 120 millions.

Table II. ESTIMATES OF WORLD POPULATION BY CONTINENTAL
DIVISIONS, 1650–1950

	Estimated Population (Millions)				
	1650	1750	1850	1900	1950
World total . . .	470	694	1,091	1,550	2,406
Africa	100	100	100	120	199
America	8	11	59	144	328
North of Rio Grande .	*1*	*1*	*26*	*81*	*166*
South of Rio Grande .	*7*	*10*	*33*	*63*	*162*
Asia (exc. Asiatic U.S.S.R.)	257	437	656	857	1,272
Europe and Asiatic U.S.S.R.	103	144	274	423	594
Oceania	2	2	2	6	13

Source: *Population Bulletin No. 1*, United Nations, December 1951.

changes in current vital rates but of the persistence of
some existing rates. This is the best approach at the
start. Demographers have, moreover, done intensive
research to discover which are the more fundamental and
stable statistics, on the grounds that the more stable
existing rates provide the best basis for extrapolation.

In the absence of all independent evidence this approach
would no doubt be the best. But it must be observed
that other evidence may well be brought to refute what
is not a completely logical assumption; for a rate (say the
birth-rate) may have been stable for fifty years or more,
and yet be due for a change (e.g., if all potential mothers
are known to have suffered from famine in youth) which
if not strictly predictable can at least be thought likely;
and the same is true of net reproduction rate, or the size
of family rate, or whatever statistic is being used. This
somewhat laborious warning is necessary to prevent too
ready an acceptance of whatever happens to be the
fashionable basis of extrapolation.

3

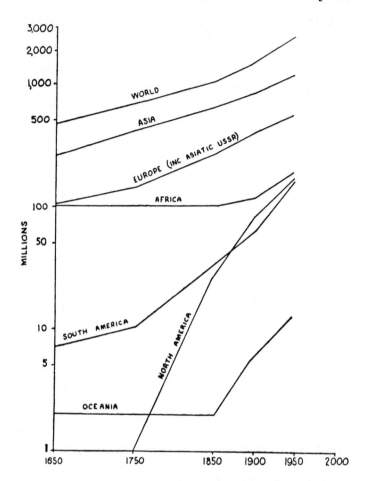

Diagram I. THE GROWTH OF WORLD POPULATION
BY CONTINENTAL DIVISIONS

Source: *Population Bulletin No. 1*, United Nations, December 1951.

There are, indeed, *two* weaknesses about any extrapolation of trends. First the errors in the basic estimates and the doubts engendered thereby. Secondly, the doubts created by the fact that in the last analysis we just do not know how many babies future generations will have, nor whether those generations will behave in the least as their predecessors have behaved, or even as they behaved themselves in earlier years; the same argument applies, though with rather less force, to their rate of dying. Mortality may be analysed under several headings. There are the deaths taking place soon after birth owing to the non-viability of the organism, there are the "normal" deaths for any environment which are an increasing function of age (from the age of about ten years onwards in Great Britain), and there are the more or less hazardous deaths due to accidents, epidemics and wars. All three are in different degrees statistically predictable for a given set of circumstances, but improvements in the different types of mortality may take place at discontinuous and at rather unpredictable rates.

Evidently, if there is a very great stability of behaviour over recent years, it is not too unreasonable to assume that this stability is quite likely to persist. But the further ahead the extrapolation is carried the greater the uncertainty attached to the hypothetical prediction; and in fact extrapolations of several centuries ahead are more or less senseless in view of the uncertainties involved.

For example, the latest available estimates[1] show that the population of the world has been changing at an *average* rate of change, cumulatively, of rather less than 1 per cent per annum (0·9 per cent per annum, or 9 per thousand) for the fifty years 1900–50. World population has been estimated at 1,550 millions in 1900 and 2,406

[1] See *Population Bulletin No. 1*, United Nations, December 1951.

millions in 1950 (see Table II) from which this rate of change has been deduced (see also Diagram I). A simple assumption, and one that may well be justified, is that the rate of change for *world* population over the next half-century will remain at approximately the same average; or in graphical terms that total world population will rise at the same slope, on a logarithmic scale, in the future as in the past. The several parts of world population have been increasing at varying rates, so this assumption is only justified if the very high rates of increase in some large portions of the globe slow down, as well as being offset by continued decline in the rates of increase experienced elsewhere.

According to the estimates given in Table II world population totalled 470 millions in 1650, a figure which statisticians have ventured to compare with 350 millions in the year A.D. 0, and two humans only (Adam and Eve) in 25,000 B.C.[1] However that may be, the average annual rate of increase in population from 1650 onwards has exceeded any previous long-period world rates, so far as these can be guessed. Moreover, the rate has increased with each half-century. From 1650 to 1850 the average was about 0·4 per cent (4 per thousand); from 1850 to 1900 about 7 per thousand, and from 1900 to 1950, as already seen, 9 per thousand.

But the rates of growth have varied very much in different parts of the world. The average annual rate of growth for the different regions over a recent period (1920–50) is shown in Table III.

The estimates suggest that American population (apart from the small population of Oceania) is the one that has advanced the most astonishingly in the first half of the twentieth century. South American population has

[1] *Ibid.*, pp. 1–2.

Table III

Region	Reliability of Estimates	Annual Average Rate of Growth, 1920–50 (%)
World	Mixed	0·9
Africa	Poor	1·3
America	Mixed	1·5
North (of Rio Grande) . .	Good	1·3
South (of Rio Grande) . .	Fair	1·9
Asia (excluding Asiatic U.S.S.R.)	Poor on the whole	0·8
Near East	Poor	1·0
S. Central	Fair	1·1
Japan	Good	1·4
Rest of Far East . . .	Poor	0·5
Europe (and Asiatic U.S.S.R.) .		
N.W. Central . . .	Good	0·6
Southern	Good	0·9
Eastern (and Asiatic U.S.S.R.)	Fair	0·7
Oceania.	Good	1·4

Source: *World Population Trends 1920–47*, Population Studies No. 3, United Nations, December 1949.

advanced by the amazing annual percentage of 1·9, and North American by 1·3 per cent per annum (over thirty years). It is important to reiterate the caution that the statement about North America rests on far firmer foundations than the statement about South America, where the margins of error for these estimates are much higher. But accepting the statistical picture, for the moment, as broadly correct, it would appear that America and not Asia is the continent of "teeming" millions. If America's current rate of increase in population continued to the end of the present century that continent would contain 732 million souls (316 millions in the U.S.A. and Canada), and perhaps form a higher percentage of the world total than to-day. It would, of course, be rash in the extreme to predict that any such development will take place.

Annual rates of growth in population may very well
decline in some parts of the world and increase violently,
at least temporarily, in others. Some of these changes
for the world taken as a whole are likely, however, to
cancel each other out.

§ 2. *Vital Rates for Different Regions.* The natural increase
of world population was not only greater in the first half
of the twentieth than in the previous half-centuries; it
appeared to be accelerating in every "normal" period.
For example, natural increase in the years 1946–48 was
somewhere between 1·1 and 1·4 per cent per annum, while
in the years 1936–38 it had been below 1·4 per cent, and
perhaps as low as 0·8 per cent (more exact estimates are
impossible, and "normal" has a relative meaning only).

Over the world as a whole the natural rate of increase
in the years 1946–48 was due to a birth-rate averaging
some 36 per thousand, and a death-rate averaging somewhere between 22 and 25 per thousand. These average
world rates, both birth and death, greatly exceeded the
rate for Europe or North America.

The regions of the world may be divided into three
distinct groups.[1] For Group I the birth-rate was about
22 and the death-rate 12, giving an annual rate of increase
of 10 per thousand. The group as a whole had a much
lower birth-rate than the other groups, but also a much
lower death-rate. But its natural rate of increase was
much greater than it had been in the recorded past.
Fears for a decline of, or stability in, the populations of
these regions sprang from a persistent decline in the birth-

[1] Group I consists of north-west, central and southern Europe,
North America (as defined in the table) and Oceania; Group II of
Latin America, Japan, Eastern Europe and Asiatic U.S.S.R.; and
Group III of Africa, Near East, South Central Asia and remaining
Far East.

rate. The increase in that rate that followed World War II was held by many observers to be due to purely temporary causes.

Within Group II, which included about 22 per cent of world population, the rates varied very widely. Some of its countries had death-rates in the range 15–17 per thousand, and its birth-rates varied from 28 in Southern Europe to 40 in South America. Its death-rates were on average moderate, neither low nor high (in relation to the world average), but still likely to decline. Its birth-rate was on average fairly high, though lower than the higher figures estimated for Group III, so that its natural rate of increase was 1·5 per cent per annum.

Group III, which was by far the largest (58 per cent of world population in 1950), was the group of both high death-rates and very high birth-rates. The latter ranged from 40 to 45 per thousand, while the death-rates varied from 25 to 30 in Africa to 30 to 35 in the Near East. The natural rate of increase was lower than in Group II, at about 1·2 per cent (12 per thousand).

Thus we have:

Table IV

	% of World Popln. (1950)	Natural Increase %		Hypothetical 1950–80 rates per thousand	
		1946–48	1920–50	"High"	"Low"
Group I (low birth- and death-rates) .	20·2	10	9	10	4
Group II (medium birth- and death-rates) . . .	22·2	15	11	19	10
Group III (high birth- and death-rates) .	57·6	12	8	13	7
World . .	100·0	12	9	14	7

Source: *Population Bulletin No. 1*, United Nations, December 1951.

While the natural rate of increase has risen for the world as a whole, it has been rising for Group III faster even than for Group II, and much faster than for Group I.

For Group I a natural increase of 10 per cent would be "high" over the thirty years to 1980; for Group II a "high" rate would be 19; for Group III perhaps 13 or a little higher, according to the views of the United Nations' statisticians. The differences are due to the demographical history of the countries in the three groups; Group II countries have the most obvious power of increase in the next few decades, because their death-rates may well continue to fall faster than their birth-rates. Group III may, however, still prove to be able to reduce its death-rates, and the "high" estimate of 13 looks too low in the light of medical developments. If we put in a "high" figure of 15, this might be nearer the possibilities. Similarly each group has its appropriate "low" estimate.

On these assumptions world population would be 3,000 millions in 1980 ("low" estimate) or 3,600 millions ("high" estimate), all the "highs" and all the "lows" being assumed to operate together. By using the same methods world population in A.D. 2000 would be between 3,416 and 4,792 millions; these figures merely illustrate the effects of applying a fixed rate of increase over a long period. The most that can be said is that no present observer would be surprised if world population were as high as 4,000 millions fifty years hence. It might be a great deal higher than this. On the other hand, birth-rates may fall much more rapidly than anticipated, in which case world population at the end of this century may be no more than 3,000 millions. This is not to say that there is any particular likelihood of its being between these figures. The important point is the order of magnitude of the increase that *may* take place, which on these figures is from 1,000 to 2,400 millions.

The immediate problem for the world is to find in the next fifty years food and other resources for perhaps nearly twice as many *extra* people as were added to the world's peoples during the preceding half-century. Evidently if these very crude projections prove to be at all near the truth, the task of world agricultural expansion and perhaps reorganization will be by no means a small one, and vast social changes may be one necessary condition of meeting the increased needs of the world. (See § 7.)

§ 3. *Reproduction Rates.*   So far only the simplest population rate—the percentage rate of change itself—has been considered.   Changes in birth-rates and death-rates were the first refinement to be introduced; thus extrapolations could be based upon assumptions of continuing the trends in these rates.   But these in turn were considered too crude in the 1930's, since they ignored the age distribution and the proportions of women of child-bearing age in the population.

The purpose of the device known as the net reproduction rate was to eliminate the so-called "distorting" effects of the age-structure of the population.[1]   The surviving girls who would succeed each 1,000 girls born, on the basis of current fertility and mortality rates, were calculated for each specific age [2] (for females the N.R.R. on this basis was 810 per thousand for Great Britain in 1935–38).   On the basis of the low (maternal) N.R.R.

[1] See section III of Appendix 3 to the Royal Commission on Population Report (Cmd. 7695, June 1949).
[2] *Ibid.* This rate differed considerably from the male rate, i.e., the "paternal" instead of the "maternal" rate, owing to the excess of males over females in that period.

some very gloomy forecasts were made, extrapolations of
this particular rate being used to demonstrate that
British and other North-West European populations were
doomed to decline; or "doomed to die out", in the phrase
invented by Dr. Kuczynski. This, indeed, must logically
be the fate of any population with a N.R.R. below 1.
The statement that such a population was "doomed to
die out" was mathematically correct, but no more so than
the statement that a population with a tendency to

Table V. NET REPRODUCTION RATES FOR SPECIFIC COUNTRIES
1939 AND 1944–49.

	U.S.	England & Wales	Belgium	Denmark	Finland	Norway	Sweden
1939	0·992	0·808	0·859	0·940	1·040	0·849	0·830
1944	1·171	0·996	0·851	1·242	1·036	1·073	1·140
1945	1·144	0·909	0·879	1·297	1·245	1·075	1·176
1946	1·359	1·103	1·022	1·319	1·382	1·221	1·161
1947	1·524	1·205	1·002	1·269	1·408	1·164	1·133
1948	1·462	1·070	0·996	—	1·403	1·126	—
1949	—	1·023	—	—	—	—	—
1950	—	0·986	—	—	—	—	—

Source: United Nations, *Demographic Yearbook 1949–50.* For England
and Wales 1949 and 1950—*Annual Abstract of Statistics*, No. 89, 1952.

increase by nearly 1 per cent was doomed to disaster.
Both statements are based upon a long-term extrapolation
of trends, but the assumption that such trends will continue indefinitely is unjustified. Trends depend upon
human habits and institutions; these endure, sometimes
through most catastrophic shocks. But human habits
can also change, and the brief recorded history of population includes some notable examples of modification in
birth- and death-rates, and for that matter in the net
reproduction rate as well. Even within a decade the net
reproduction rate varied by as much as 40 or 50 per

cent in some countries, as may be seen from Table V. The years illustrated by the table happen, it is true, to include the period of World War II, but almost equally violent short-term fluctuations could be shown if other years had been chosen, and in any case the figures establish the limited point that twentieth-century populations have the power to vary their rates of increase substantially within short periods ; so far as the reproduction rate is concerned, the one lesson that experience teaches us is that it is not necessarily constant.   About the same time as female reproduction rates (gross and net) began to reveal considerable instability, demographers discovered that these rates were open to several objections as a basis for forecasting.   Net reproduction rates, calculated as surviving girls born to mothers, fluctuate because of changes in the marriage frequency.   Such changes may, or may not, be of a temporary character; in the well-known case of World War II an unforeseen rise in marriage frequencies, due to marked changes in social behaviour, upset the stability of the reproduction rate.   Or, again, the female net reproduction rate may be misleading if, for more or less accidental historical reasons, there is a surplus of women and so a low marriage frequency among them ; the net reproduction rate will rise over the years as this surplus readjusts itself even though fertility among married women stays constant.

Demographers have therefore looked for other evidence of a pattern of stability; in the case of Britain in particular, as will be seen, they have developed the concept of "completed family size".   For the world as a whole such refinements, whether useful or not, are quite impracticable for lack of sufficient information on the age distribution of mothers, nuptiality and other necessary particulars.

§ 4. *Logistic Curves and their Limitations.* At one time it
was hoped that the fitting of mathematical curves to data
of the total size of population would help to solve, in a
rather simple way, the problem of how to project what
different populations would "naturally" tend to become.
If it can be assumed (which it cannot) that the rate of
reproduction remains constant, then ultimately the size
of a population increases (or decreases) in a geometric
progression.[1]   On the other hand, any such logarithmic
rate of increase must be curbed because of a deficiency in
the rate of increase in the supply of food or of some other
necessity, or because of the simple fact of spatial limitation, so that the assumed rate of growth may further be
assumed to have a diminishing rate itself.   The growth
equation must, then, be modified, and a "logistic" S-
shaped curve will represent the projection.[2]

In the early 1920's Yule worked out an estimate of the
projected population for England and Wales based on a
logistic curve, and Pearl and Reed produced similar
calculations for America.   Bowley calculated the future
size of the British population on the basis of mortality
rates (those for England and Wales 1910–12) and the
average number of births from 1921–23.   According to
Yule's logistic curve the population for England and
Wales should have become 51 millions by 1951 (it was
actually 44 millions) and he regarded Bowley's estimate
of 49 millions by 1971 as much too low.   But, as Bowley
pointed out, the logistic was not the only curve that could
reasonably be fitted to the data for the past populations
of the different countries.

---

[1] and [2] See Cox, 1952, p. 82 ff.   If the population at a moment of
time is P_t the first assumption can be expressed as $P_t = Ce^{rt}$ where
C and r (the rate of growth) are constants, t is time, and e is the ex-
ponential; r will be reduced by a value that is a function of P_t if a
ceiling of some sort is further assumed.

Mr. Cox remarks [1] that it would "not be impossible to obtain plausible results by joining two or more logistics together or by using more tortuous curves", but he adds that "not much confidence could be placed in their predictive power unless special regard was had in choosing them to the present age-structure of the population and the current tendencies of birth rates and death rates". But can any confidence be placed in these curves even if Mr. Cox's condition is fulfilled? The whole weight of the argument once more rests upon the discovery of an alleged "current tendency" in the habits of reproduction and dying, and on an act of faith (or reason) that any such tendency will continue in the future.

The factors affecting births and deaths are economic, sociological, agricultural, political and so on, and embrace all the material and spiritual influences that affect human behaviour. Many different disciplines have to be consulted. The assumptions made finally demand an act of choice, or, indeed, of political judgment.

The logistic curve has not provided very successful projections because it was based upon some over-simplified assumptions. It seems probable that there is no single mathematical "law of growth" that is followed by human populations, or if there is a simplifying principle of this kind, it remains to be discovered.

§ 5. *Population Projections of the 1940's.* Since earlier attempts to study population growth had proved so unsuccessful it might be thought that economists and statisticians would refuse to risk their reputations upon further projections based upon necessarily arbitrary assumptions. But the pressure of necessity is too great; there are many practical reasons why projections of

[1] *Ibid.*, p. 88.

population should be required. Most writers of any repute distinguish between "projections" and "predictions", and to make the distinction valid offer several projections each based on a different set of hypotheses. But the possible number of hypotheses is, in theory, infinite. Each writer presumably selects that set of hypotheses which is in his view more probable than all the infinite sets that he neglects to mention. A projection is, therefore, a prediction—with an extra danger sign attached.

A simplifying principle in the history of population growth began to be discerned in the 1930's and became accepted doctrine as the basis of the projections worked out in the next decade. The principle might be called the theory of three demographic stages in civilization. The first stage, that of more primitive societies, is a so-called "natural" stage of high birth-rates and high death-rates; this was the stage from which Western European peoples began to free themselves towards the end of the eighteenth century. The second stage is that which follows the introduction of some medical, sanitary and hygienic improvements, and is a stage of falling death-rates with birth-rates still remaining high. This stage is one of rapid natural increase. The third stage is begun when urbanization, social ambition and other factors have combined to reduce the size of families by reduction in the birth-rate, and is finally reached when birth-rates are falling faster than death-rates. The ultimate consequence of this stage is a falling population.[1]

The three stages theory is apparently founded upon the history of growth of the Western European communities from about 1790 to 1940. Other populations have, more-

[1] The three stages correspond roughly to the three Groups—Group III being in the main in stage one, Group II in stage two, and Group I in stage three.

over, appeared, in respect of declining death-rates, to follow suit, and the three stages theory has become a kind of orthodoxy; for example, it is often assumed that a country like Japan will pass through a period of rapid expansion, and then, like Western European countries that have been industrialized, experience a falling birth-rate and reach relative stability of total numbers.

The theory of the three stages underlay the interesting projections of population that were made by Professor Notestein and his colleagues in the 1940's. They were careful to observe that they had no proof that history would repeat itself in the manner that the theory implies, but in the absence of any better guide they turned to past experience, and built their projections on the assumption that each major section of the world's population would progress more or less consistently through each phase of development.

According to the three stages theory the world's population problem is essentially acute but short-term. As each "backward" country, or region, moves from the primitive to the second stage its population will increase alarmingly, that is to say much faster than it can, with existing techniques, increase its supplies of food. Each country will in turn seem to have to face a period of population crisis such as was experienced by Britain in the early nineteenth century and is being faced by Japan in the twentieth. There will be problems of emigration, of raising capital from abroad, of imports and of urbanization at home. But fortunately a third stage will eventually supervene, and if the critical stage, the hump as it were, can be passed, an easier period will lie ahead, as family limitation begins to have numerical effect.

This general picture of the future of world population growth is still, perhaps, the best that we have, but there are several flaws in it of marked importance to economists. The major difficulty is that in this, as in some other population theories, movements in population growth are treated as independent variables, or as variables dependent only upon such relatively simple factors as "medical improvements" and "family limitation". In the real world even these two simple factors sum up and include complex developments, and furthermore many other factors, including economic, may be relevant to the extent to which these factors operate.[1]

The three stages theory is based upon historical experience, and upon the belief that European experience will be repeated for other nations. But there is a sense in which the only lesson of history in this matter is that of the uniqueness of the circumstances surrounding each development. The most striking conclusion, to be derived from Table II (and Diagram I), is that world population history has in a very special sense been unique, and on this point there must be general agreement. There has been no repetition and there are no precedents to apply of a simple and direct kind.

At least four major factors affected European development, which may not again be present—the existence of sparsely inhabited land to exploit in temperate zones of climate, the discovery of raw materials to mine in sufficient quantities to support a particular type of material urban civilization, the successful introduction of the social and political changes that enabled hygiene to play its part in reducing death-rates (as well as striking medical

---

[1] Of one version of the Malthusian theory it is often said that it ignores the "middle term"; the (geometrical) increase in population is treated as quite independent of the (arithmetical) increase in food. In fact the important point is just how the two increases are interrelated. This is a similar criticism to that here developed of the "three stages" theory.

advances in attacking epidemic diseases), and technical developments such as railways and roads which required large labour forces to construct and maintain. These are only examples and not an exhaustive list. The point is that these, and other important economic and social factors, are very unlikely to repeat themselves; the question at issue is whether there will be sufficient substitutes for them. If there are, then backward populations may develop on much the same lines as the European populations which first exploited the resources of industrial civilization. But there is no certainty that populations will automatically repeat these developments.

To begin with, the movement from stage 1 to stage 2 is taking place under very different circumstances from those that ruled when the Western world was first heavily industrialized. The decline in the death-rates then, even now not fully understood, certainly depended in part upon social as well as medical improvements. Now that advanced education is available to administrators medical improvements may be introduced into "backward" areas with little change in the social arrangements.

The movement from stage 2 to stage 3 is even more critical, and still less likely to be a simple repetition of the earlier European decline in fertility.[1] The desire to limit family size arises only in certain social circumstances (again, not fully understood even for Europe), and those circumstances may well not prevail in the expanding areas of the twentieth century. On the contrary, it is possible that quite different factors may operate. Recent studies of Ceylon,[2] for example, an area with high birth-rates and comparatively low death-rates, show that while there

[1] Those who have predicted a movement from stage 2 to stage 3 have leaned rather heavily on an argument from analogy with the demographic history of Japan.
[2] Taeuber, 1949, p. 302.

4

Table VI

Continents and Countries	Population (millions)			Annual % Rate of Growth	
	1900	1939	1949	1900–1949	1939–1949
Africa					
Egypt . . .	10·3	16·6	20·0	1·3	1·9
Gold Coast . .	1·6	3·5	3·7	2·1	0·6
Union South Africa	4·7	10·2	12·1	2·0	1·7
Others . . .	124·1	144·7	162·1	0·4	1·1
TOTAL . .	140·7	175·0	197·9	0·6	1·3
America					
Argentina . .	4·8	14·4	16·8	2·8	1·6
Brazil . . .	17·0	40·3	49·3	2·2	2·1
Canada . . .	5·2	11·6	13·2	2·0	1·6
Chile . . .	2·9	4·9	5·7	1·4	1·5
Colombia . .	3·5	8·9	11·0	2·4	2·1
Cuba . . .	1·6	4·5	5·2	2·7	1·5
Ecuador . .	1·4	2·9	3·4	1·9	1·1
United States .	76·0	130·9	149·2	1·4	1·4
Honduras . .	0·5	1·1	1·3	2·1	1·7
Jamaica . .	0·8	1·2	1·4	1·0	1·6
Mexico . .	13·6	19·4	24·4	0·9	2·3
Peru . . .	4·6	6·9	8·2	1·0	1·7
Puerto Rico . .	1·0	1·8	2·2	1·5	2·1
El Salvador . .	1·0	1·7	2·2	1·4	2·6
Uruguay . .	0·9	2·1	2·4	2·2	1·4
Venezuela . .	2·5	3·6	4·6	0·9	2·5
Others . . .	13·7	17·8	20·3	0·7	1·2
TOTAL . .	151·0	274·0	320·8	1·5	1·6
Asia					
Burma . .	11·8	16·0	18·3	0·8	1·4
Ceylon . . .	3·5	5·9	7·3	1·4	2·1
China . . .	357·3	450·0	463·5	0·6	0·3
Korea and Formosa	·13·2	27·8	36·3	2·0	3·8
India and Pakistan	282·5	380·0	420·4	0·8	1·0
Japan . . .	43·8	70·9	82·1	1·3	1·5
Philippines . .	7·5	16·2	20·4	2·0	2·3
Thailand . .	7·8	15·0	18·0	1·7	1·8
Indonesia . .	35·0	69·4	72·0	1·7	0·3
Others . . .	76·5	110·8	115·2	0·9	0·4
TOTAL . .	838·9	1,162·0	1,253·5	0·8	0·8

Table VI.—continued

Continents and Countries	Population (millions)			Annual % Rate of Growth	
	1900	1930	1949	1900 – 1949	1939– 1949
Europe					
Belgium . .	6·7	8·4	8·6	0·6	0·2
Bulgaria . .	3·9	6·3	7·2	1·3	1·4
Czechoslovakia .	12·1	14·7	12·5	0·5	– 1·6
Denmark . .	2·6	3·8	4·2	0·9	1·0
Finland . .	2·6	3·7	4·0	0·9	0·8
France . .	40·1	41·3	41·6	0·1	0·1
Hungary . .	6·8	9·2	9·2	0·8	—
Ireland. .	3·2	2·9	3·0	– 0·2	0·3
Italy . .	33·4	43·1	46·0	0·7	0·7
Netherlands . .	5·1	8·8	10·0	1·4	1·3
Norway . .	2·2	3·0	3·2	0·8	0·7
Portugal . .	5·4	7·6	8·5	0·9	1·1
Spain . .	18·5	25·5	28·0	0·8	0·9
Sweden . .	5·1	6·3	7·0	0·6	1·0
Switzerland . .	3·3	4·2	4·6	0·7	0·9
United Kingdom .	37·9	47·8	50·4	0·6	0·6
TOTAL . .	188·9	236·6	248·0	0·6	0·5
Others . . .	100·0	165·9	144·8	1·3	– 1·4
U.S.S.R. . .	126·0	170·5	200·0	0·8	1·6
TOTAL (Europe)	414·9	573·0	592·8	0·8	0·3
Oceania					
Australia . .	3·8	7·0	7·9	1·6	1·3
New Zealand .	0·8	1·6	1·9	1·8	1·7
Others . . .	1·6	2·4	2·6	1·0	0·8
TOTAL . .	6·2	11·0	12·4	1·5	1·2
World . . .	1,551·7	2,195·0	2,377·4	0·9	0·8

Sources: World Health Organization, *Epidemiological and Vital Statistics Report*, April 1951, Table II. United Nations, *Demographic Yearbook 1949–50*.

is no apparent difference in the birth-rates of the large and small cities (Colombo and the rest), there is a higher than average birth-rate in the rural areas. But parts of Ceylon which were once fertile are under-populated, and to win more food these parts must again be inhabited. As, further, Ceylon has little immediate prospect of rapid industrialization, more of its energies must be directed to raising food. It cannot expect to gain an "automatic" reduction of birth-rates as people move to the towns, as to some extent a reverse flow is necessary, nor is there sufficient time for the small family pattern to spread from cities to rural districts. Thus, if a demographic crisis is to be averted, as Irene Taeuber points out, there must be a *direct* development of the small family pattern in the rural areas, which means that Ceylon's demographic evolution must vary considerably from the Western precedent. But Ceylon's case is paralleled all over Asia. The problem is how to populate the, at present, badly irrigated areas without worsening instead of improving the ratio of population to fertile acreage.

Unless it can be assumed that there is a unique relationship between population change, social and economic reorganization, and the population change again, it cannot be deduced that each stage of population development will be followed by the same type of successor. The projections for different parts of the world may turn out to be approximately correct, but there may be many surprises yet in store. The most knowledgeable forecasters in 1950–51 varied in their guesses of future world population in the year 2000 by a factor of at least 25 per cent (a figure of 3,000 millions being mentioned about as frequently as 4,000 millions). If the higher figure is used, the increase in population in half a century would amount to 1,600 millions on 2,400 millions, that is 2 persons more for every 3 alive in 1950.

No great importance can therefore be attached to our own rough guess of an increase of something like 1,600 millions.   The movement in the sum total of world population is the result of varying rates of change in many different countries, and the reasons for these changes in the past are not so certain that predictions about the future have any serious reliability.   All that can be said is that for the world as a whole a very large increase in numbers between 1950 and 2000 seems to be likely, and that the increase will very likely be greater than the whole world population existing in 1900.

§ 6. *Differing Percentage Rates of Increase.*   While there seems to be no reliable general "law of population" on which to base prognostications about the future of the world as a whole, certain key statistics can be worked out for individual states which may be thought to throw some light on the problems of the next fifty years.   In Table VI recent percentage rates of change in total populations are shown in contrast with the rates of change for the same areas recorded for the first half of the twentieth century. In many cases the more recent change considerably exceeds the earlier average.   (Only those countries for which fairly reliable census figures are available have been shown.)

Many parts of the world have annual percentage rates of change that clearly cannot be sustained for any long period of time because of all sorts of limiting factors, including the obvious one of physical living-space.   Any country which is increasing at a natural rate of 2 per cent per annum or more (Puerto Rico for example) would seem quite likely to be heading for a food supply problem unless it can either (*a*) export enough to increase its food imports, (*b*) increase its farm productivity by a very high factor, or (*c*) arrange for large-scale emigration (legal or illegal). In the actual case of Puerto Rico emigration seems to be the solution adopted. It would be very satisfying if a simple generalization could be reached, namely, that any percentage rate of change above some critical level (say $1\frac{1}{2}$ per cent) represents a "catastrophic" increase, and implies a crisis in the affairs of the country concerned. Unfortunately no such tidy division of the world is at all legitimate.

For consider the countries which do in fact, undeniably, have a rate of change that cannot for ever be maintained. There are at least three groups among those above the 2 per cent level. First are the still "empty" countries with agricultural land far from fully exploited by Western European standards. These include Australia, New Zealand and Argentina. Their increases are in two cases due to immigration, not to natural increase. But what is sauce for the goose is sauce for the gander, and if 2 per cent is too much *on principle* it is too much for these countries as well as others. In fact this group of countries is demographically not ill situated. More population will strengthen them economically by improving their industries and their agriculture.

The second group of countries are the large semi-tropical countries like Brazil, Algeria, Colombia and Mexico which, too, in certain favourable conditions, may well support much larger populations than they do at present. Their way ahead is not so plain as that of the new (mainly temperate zone) countries, but granted that tropical agriculture can be increasingly exploited their futures would seem to be reasonably secure. Finally there are the small, already crowded, territories like Ceylon and Trinidad, islands and small states, where the density of numbers to land has given rise already to urgent social problems. But for these countries, too, the immediate outlook is far less certainly unhappy than is sometimes depicted.[1]

Again and again it is necessary to remind ourselves not to confuse the long-term *impossibility* of certain rates of increase with the short-term *desirability* of these (or even higher) rates. It is all very well to write (of Ceylon for instance) that "a rate of population increase of even 2·5 per cent per year *far into the future*" would lead to inconceivably high figures. This is beside the point, in relation to policy for the next fifty years. It would seem that a rate of increase of 2·5 or 3·0 per cent, or any other percentage, is perfectly in order until such time as the present seven million inhabitants of the island are increased to whatever is the highest figure that the island can, in modern conditions, sustain. Certainly we cannot be sure that 2·5 per cent is too fast a rate of increase for Ceylon, or Australia, or New Zealand, or Brazil, unless we study first their economic and social possibilities.

Thus, the world possibilities of a large increase of population depend partly upon how the relevant, but complex, problems of the differing rates of change affecting different national groups are solved. How great an increase the world can support can be calculated in several ways, according to the way in which the increase is distributed.

There is no sound basis for projecting world population ahead far into the future regardless of the economic and agricultural developments that are expected to take place. Moreover, it must be remembered that changes in total

[1] *Ceylon:* "Potentially the population problem is acute, but there are agricultural areas for expansion, lands which can be more intensively utilized, and some industrial opportunities. Ceylon has enough time to undertake the research essential to discover . . . how to solve her population problem by inducing a reduction in the size of families." Taeuber, 1949, p. 303.

population for particular areas depend upon migration as well as upon births and deaths.

Approximately, then, it may be thought that the large increase in world population up to A.D. 2000 will divide itself between the groups at rates similar to those estimated for 1950–80 in Table IV. A rough alternative guess may be made by simple extrapolation of the lines shown in Diagram I. Many refinements can be introduced into these calculations for individual countries, but they are based on equally arbitrary assumptions; for a first view of the possibilities the above projections may suffice.

§ 7. *World Population and Food Supplies.* (*a*) Great alarm has been expressed from time to time at the rate of growth of world population especially in relation to the food supplies likely to be available.[1] This anxiety has been intensified by the Malthusian theories of population, which will be discussed in a later chapter. The present section will be used to afford a brief first view of the orders of magnitude of the problem under discussion.

Leaving aside, for the moment, the structural economic difficulties,[2] one fact is indisputable, namely, that there is

[1] For example, Michael Roberts opened his book, *The Estate of Man,* 1951, with the remark that:

(p. 13) "If all the 56 million square miles of the earth's land surface were shared out equally among its 2,350 million people, we would each have about 15 acres, including roughly 5 acres of jungle, or forest, about 4 acres of dry desert, another 2 acres of semi-arid land and 2 acres of polar snow. . . . Over the world as a whole, the area actually cultivated amounts to just about one and a half acres per person. . . . A century ago, the estate would have been twice as large. . . . At the present rate . . . each of us is losing about an acre every ten years."

(p. 18) "Wheat is of crucial importance: it is the staple food of nations such as Britain and Belgium which depend largely on imported grain; it is the alternative to which the Asiatic countries turn as they outstrip their own supplies of rice. . . ."

[2] The structural difficulties include those arising in the production of food, the organization of farming, the degree of education and state

no *physical* difficulty to be seen in the way of increasing food supplies at least as fast as population over the next fifty years. Enough is known, on a sufficiently firm basis, to state categorically that for that period at least there is enough land and enough knowledge of techniques already ascertained to support a world population that increases at nearly I per cent per annum for another fifty years. Table VII illustrates the increase in yields per hectare and per person secured in many parts of the world after the war-time setbacks.

Professor Le Gros Clark has surely summed up the position correctly with the remark [1]:

> "The knowledge that we have is, in our view, sufficient to guarantee the increased agricultural production we need during this century; after that the outlook is unpredictable."

The point is that the knowledge *we have* is sufficient; no allowance need be made for inventions or unforeseen improvements in agricultural technique. As far as sheer physical quantity of food is concerned, to keep the world in the year 2000 no hungrier on average than it was in 1939, and perhaps a little less hungry than it was in 1951, the existing techniques, applied on a wider scale than in the middle of the century, would suffice.

Two major economic matters have to be considered. First there is the immense question of the economic and social structures necessary to ensure that the potentially fertile areas of the world are in fact brought into

policies in regard to agricultural development, technical education and nutrition, and also the complex problems arising in the distribution of food. Among the latter are difficulties due to the distribution of agriculture as between continents, and also of course both between and within individual countries.

[1] Le Gros Clark, 1951, p. 1.

Table VII. AGRICULTURAL PRODUCTIVITY BY CONTINENTS AND FOR THE WORLD PRE-WAR AND 1947–48

(In Metric Tons)

	Yield per Hectare					Yield per Person in Agriculture				
	Pre-war	1947–48	1950–51	1947–48 as % of pre-war	1950–51 as % of pre-war	Pre-war	1947–48	1950–51	1947–48 as % of pre-war	1950–51 as % of pre-war
Africa	0·77	0·73	0·83	95	108	0·12	0·12	0·14	100	117
Asia	1·26	1·20	1·19	95	94	0·24	0·22	0·23	92	96
Europe	1·51	1·34	1·60	89	106	1·04	0·88	1·02	85	98
North and Central America	1·07	1·50	1·53	140	143	1·80	2·57	2·46	143	137
South America	1·28	1·39	1·31	109	102	0·58	0·48	0·45	83	78
Oceania	1·06	1·20	1·47	113	139	1·94	2·38	2·28	123	118
World	1·24	1·30	1·36	105	110	0·42	0·42	0·44	100	105

Data based on the production of eight crops, wheat, rye, oats, barley, rice, maize, sugar and potatoes, expressed on a wheat basis.

Source: F.A.O., *Food and Agricultural Statistics*, Washington, September 1949.

Data for 1950 calculated on same basis and using same weights.

NOTE.—In Africa, and to some extent in Asia, the low figure for production per person in agriculture arises in part from the fact that these eight crops play a lesser part in the food production of these continents. No reliable figures are, however, available for the other crops.

cultivation, or improved in yield, before any major disasters occur in the way of famine or economic breakdown. Second is the question of cost. Even if cost per unit of output does not rise exorbitantly, the conservatism of peasant and farming communities, and difficulties of distribution of food due to the division of the world into national states (two political factors), may slow down the effective rate of increase.

More intensive application of fertilizers, and the wider use of improved techniques, would substantially increase the output of land that is already cultivated. Mankind will thus not necessarily become worse off, in the next fifty years, merely because of its continued expansion in numbers. But the required increase in demand implies in turn adequate channels for distributing the output of agriculture. A closer analysis of the distribution of food is therefore necessary if any realistic impression is to be formed of the economic pressures likely to be set up by the expansion of population.

Nutritionally, as in other ways, the world is, as Mr. Colin Clark once observed, a wretchedly poor place. The point can be established in two ways—on the basis of over-all statistics of food consumption per head of population in different countries, and by looking for special symptoms of malnutrition. Neither method is wholly conclusive nor satisfactory, for reasons that will appear. There are, however, sufficient facts to support the view that food consumption is either abominably or moderately insufficient for most people in most parts of the world, and that increasing populations with rising standards of living may well impose a much greater strain on the supply elasticity of agriculture than on that of any other industry except perhaps building and construction.

Out of the 1,778 million people for whom rough calculations of calories per head per day could be assessed, 1,226 millions in 1949–50 were estimated to live in countries with less than 2,400 calories per head per day average consumption.   Only 267 millions lived in countries where the average daily consumption of calories was 3,000 or better.[1]

If the average daily need of calories is about 3,000, large sections of the world's population rarely obtain so much.   Their stature, their health and their chances of life are thereby prejudiced.

The question thus becomes not merely whether food supplies can increase at the same rate as population, but whether they can increase faster.   There may be no good reason to fear that the world as a whole will be necessarily much worse off for food in the year 2000 than it was in the year 1950, but can it be any better off?   And for the population theorist this raises a supplementary and still more disturbing query: has the population of the globe *already* outrun the available subsistence?   Is the only possible remedy for the shortages that exist a reduction in the total of the existing population?

The scientific study of nutrition and the discovery of such substances as vitamins are recent developments, and no doubt much remains yet to be discovered.   Dogmatic statements as to how much an "average man" needs in the way of energy food daily, or of the forty nutritional elements at present thought necessary to maintain his organism "in balance", must be interpreted surely as relative rather than absolute in their application, however learned their source.   For medical researchers have in mind a certain standard of "health", and relate their experiments to this standard, yet the standard may

[1] *F.A.O. Yearbook 1951*, Vol. IV, Part I, Table 77, p. 161.

itself be raised if new scientific possibilities of lengthening life, or increasing human energy output, are made. The standard is in practice probably set by unconscious social assumptions.

Subject to this important qualification, the known "needs of man" may be approximately described, wide variations between individuals, and perhaps between groups, being admitted as a further possibility. In the way that our knowledge is at present organized, malnutrition is divided into three kinds: first a shortage of the energy foods, second a deficiency of any of the chemical elements necessary to balanced replacement of the human organism (i.e., replacement to a "normal" level), and, thirdly, deficiencies of the elements to such a degree as to provoke visible symptoms of disease. Thus, as an example of the first kind of shortage, if prisoners are fed on a diet of 1,000 calories a day, as in the Nazi concentration camps, they will become living skeletons and perish prematurely. The second kind of deficiency may produce no visible symptoms, but may predispose its victims to the onset of various diseases, while the third or more extreme kind will produce special diseases associated with insufficiencies of the required elements.

The third kind of deficiency would seem to be the easiest to identify, and there are certain specific diseases associated with particular shortages. Thus lack of vitamin A produces blindness, of vitamin B_1 beriberi and pellagra, of B_2 eye congestion and other diseases, of D rickets and osteomalacia.[1]

---

[1] As Mr. de Castro points out, diagnosis is not always easy. Often several vitamin deficiencies exist at once, and there are visible symptoms of the lack of necessary elements, such as digestive disorders, minor skin ailments, insomnia and so on, before the characteristic disease has appeared. There are now at least twenty vitamins identified, and a number of mineral salts and fats, all required in a balanced diet.

Shortages of vitamins A, B_1, B_2, D and C are those at present known to have the worst effect on great masses of human beings collectively.[1] Their full effects have usually been discovered as the result of some unintentional "experiment" with human beings, such as sending a ship round the globe without supplies of meat, milk and vegetables, or feeding a large section of the inhabitants of an island on polished rice, or providing the pioneers in an Amazonian rubber boom with tinned food only. From disasters due to such specialized diets much has been learnt as to the necessity of balanced feeding, and it is possible to identify broad categories of deficiency in areas of the world where no such specialized conditions exist.

Regarded from this point of view, what are the hunger areas of the world? The F.A.O. report for 1948 [2] remarked that: "As regards the energy value of the food supplies, the current situation shows that apart from Argentina, Oceania, Canada, the United States and a few European countries the food supply of any single country would be nutritionally inadequate even if distributed evenly throughout the population." The position since 1948 has not yet fundamentally changed,[3] and uneven distribution inside most countries ensures that the poorer sections of the populations concerned fare very much worse than the national average.

The hunger areas of the world fall into three classes: the low-income and densely populated countries in the Far East and the Middle East, and to a lesser degree in the Caribbean and in eastern Europe; the low-income but sparsely populated countries, chiefly in Africa and South America; and the "special areas" of hunger that crop up

[1] De Castro, 1952, p. 50.
[2] F.A.O., 1948, p. 7.
[3] F.A.O., 1952, p. 17.

all over the world, even in high-income and relatively well-fed political units. The degree of hunger or mal-nutrition varies enormously. In Chile perhaps 50 per cent of the country's inhabitants are said to get less than 2,400 calories a day. In almost every country of South America calorie intake figures were said to be very low. This fearful hunger and chronic under-nourishment occurs in a half-continent which from a demographic point of view would not appear to be ill-situated. It includes 16 per cent of the world's habitable land and only 6 per cent of the world's population. One important point is that "this hunger is nothing new"; it has come from the past, from the period of the earliest discovery of the New World.

Hunger, of course, exists in both senses of the term throughout China and India, and in some parts of Africa.

The facts as they stand neither support nor refute the view that a persistently rising population has at all times led to a worsening in food supply (apart from any allevia-tion due to the introduction of new methods of farming).

What they do show, however, is that, historically, starvation is by no means an experience occurring for the first time in recent years; it has been rife in many parts of the world for a long time. The shortages that now exist do not even seem to be worse than those of the past, except for the post-war experience for a few years of some war-devastated countries.

In certain places population *has* increased faster than food supply could be economically increased, and such increases might indeed be "independent"[1] (for instance,

[1] With regard to the "independence" of population growth the "Group of Experts" reporting to the U.N. on "Measures for the Economic Development of Under-Developed Countries" in May 1951 wrote that: "The rate of growth of population is now first and foremost a function of the extent to which medical knowledge is made available

because of the introduction of an extraneous medical improvement), and the ensuing food shortage, however temporary, might be called the consequence of the sudden spurt in population. A case of this kind that is often cited is that of British Guiana.[1] But starvation exists in regions where there has been no such sudden spurt; there is malnutrition in lands where there are ample resources of land if so organized as to meet the population's requirements. The facts do not therefore fit in with the theory that over-population is the sole cause of hunger.

There is no happy future foreseeable for an increasing world population on the scale under discussion, if social and economic institutions are not susceptible of change and adaptation. The F.A.O. as long ago as 1946 made some calculations of the percentage increase in the world production (i.e., 70 countries included in their survey) of

to the people. . . . Medical knowledge will spread, and the population will increase, whether economic development takes place or not." This is perhaps too strong, but contains an important grain of truth.

[1] In this colony the introduction of insecticides in 1945 is alleged to have resulted, in one suburb of Georgetown, in a spectacular decline in the infantile mortality rate; and for the whole of Georgetown DDT is supposed to have diminished, in the short space of a few years, the killing effect of malaria as a form of population control. For the suburb in question the birth-rate doubled between 1938-44 and 1947. (See Tizard, 1948.)

British Guiana, if these statistics were typical for the colony, may have achieved a 10 per cent annual rate of increase in the population. This has been quoted as a single example of a world-wide change towards an ever-increasing rate of growth of population. (See R. C. Cook, 1951, pp. 69 and 319, where Sir Henry Tizard's speech has been written up, but not quite accurately.)

But British Guiana (a) had a surplus of potentially cultivable land in relation to its population, (b) had absorbed East Indian immigrants in the past quite successfully, and some in the West Indies looked to it as a further outlet for possible immigration, (c) had and has substantial agricultural and mineral resources available for export, (d) had no time for social adjustments to the DDT innovation. By no stretch of language could this tiny colony of 400,000 persons in 1948 be accurately described as an instance of population pressing hard against rapidly exhausting resources of nature (of. the Year-Book of the West Indies, 1951).

certain food supplies necessary to reach its minimum nutritional targets by the year 1960. These ranged from a 12 per cent increase in sugar production to 163 per cent increase in the supply of fruit and vegetables.[1] The worst fed countries required an increase in food supplies of some 40 per cent to reach the F.A.O.'s nutritional targets for their existing populations, and of some 100 per cent to allow for their increasing populations. In the high-income countries something could be done by redistribution, but for the low-income countries production was the most essential requirement; although an even distribution of the consequent result would be just as necessary—a point perhaps not sufficiently emphasized even by the F.A.O. Both the enormous expansion of production, and the guarantees of reasonably even distribution, imply institutional growth or change in many of the seventy countries considered and co-operation between their various governments.

The nutritional "targets" laid down by the F.A.O. in 1946 have been derided by critics who pride themselves on realism and dislike an apparently altruistic proposal to give a "glass of milk to every Hottentot". But the figures just studied do not leave the question open as to which is the more realistic approach. If the nutritional targets are not attained, the scale of the crises of malnutrition and famine will be greater than any that have hitherto been experienced. It is difficult to believe realistically that these disasters will fail to spread, and

[1] The figures were:

Percentage Increases over Pre-war Food Supplies to meet 1960 Requirements

Commodity	%	Commodity	%
Cereals	21	Pulses	80
Roots and tubers	27	Fruits and vegetables	163
Sugar	12	Meat	46
Fats	34	Milk	100

that the existence of vast hordes of ill-nourished individuals in some countries, and smaller groups in others,
will not bring unpleasant consequences even to those who
at first have an adequate standard of life. Adequate food,
at least, would seem to rank high among the objectives of
international policy, although the precise standard laid
down by the F.A.O. may be challenged by some; for
there are many who would argue that the standard should
be lower than the full nutritional diet proposed by that
organization. Whatever standard is adopted (an adequate
one or a deliberately insufficient one) output and distribution have to be improved, unless population growth is
to be a principal cause of political disaster.

§ 8. *Population and Raw Materials.* What are raw materials? As distinct from manufactures, they may be defined as those goods which are acquired directly from
man's environment, without processing, for the purpose
of being worked up into products with an exchange value,
but they exclude any of those goods destined to be
consumed as food.

Raw materials are normally regarded as a different
class of commodity from foodstuffs. They include, among
organic items, cotton, wool, rubber and natural fibres such
as jute or flax. But there are some which are both raw
materials and foodstuffs, like whale oil and certain kinds
of alcohol, oilseeds and nuts, from which industrial as well
as edible products can be made. For some purposes it is
desirable to treat tobacco as a raw material, for others as
a part of "food and drink" consumption. The organic
raw materials often directly compete with food production
for land as well as for labour and capital.

A second main class of raw materials includes all the
useful minerals.

There is no complete record of world raw material production since 1900, so it is not possible to give a comprehensive estimate of the percentage increases (total and per head of population) in raw material usage that have taken place over the last half-century. But the figures shown in a graph in Chapter X below confirm the general view that the percentage increase in the use of raw materials since 1913 has greatly exceeded the percentage increase in population. (Raw materials are not shown directly in the graph, but as the "mining and manufacturing" index is some 220 per cent greater than it was in 1913 a corresponding raw material index, if it could be compiled, would probably have moved upwards by a somewhat similar rate of increase, except in so far as economies in raw materials have been effected.)

Whatever the exact figures, it is obvious that the huge rise in raw material use since the beginning of the century is out of all proportion to the increase in population. It is not, then, population as such that is pressing upon the raw material supplies of the world, but the tendency towards a greater usage per head. This might be described as an "income factor", a rise due to the general rise in real incomes. The description is only partially true, for it may be that real incomes could have been increased in a number of different ways. The increased raw material usage per head is due to an increase in real incomes by a particular developmental route.

A full analysis of that route would demand detailed statistics, analysed for several countries over a long period. For the present purpose it will suffice to pick out some outstanding reasons for the higher use of raw materials. The first one is that the highly industrialized countries, in particular the United States, have since 1918 geared their development to the principles of mass production, standardization and rapid obsolescence (critics call this conspicuous waste and protagonists call it efficiency). The modern economy relies very largely in its growth on a policy of rapid scrapping of machines and of the products of the machines.

This particular kind of economy draws more heavily each year on raw materials than one which has advanced along conservationist lines. Whether this is a good or bad thing is a somewhat debatable question. The point here is to note that it has happened.

The result of this development, and of the prodigious increase in real national income that the United States enjoyed over the thirty-five years from 1918 to 1953, has been an ever-increasing demand for raw materials in that country. In 1950 the United States used over 50 per cent of the wood pulp production of the free world. The use of "industrial lumber" only (i.e., excluding wood used as fuel) is also extremely high in the United States; in the free world generally its use is considered to be likely to rise by something of the order of 40 per cent by 1975 (on the basis of certain assumptions as to population increase and of usage per head).[1] But the use of some of the other organic materials might not increase so fast, as synthetic products, made of industrial lumber, are expected to cut down the demand for certain wool, cotton and linen goods. The possibility of organic raw materials competing against each other is important.

The uneven distribution of raw materials between different countries makes it impossible to generalize as to the future course of raw material development. It may be that fears of over-all shortages as populations increase are not fully warranted, for as the very advanced countries move on to new industries and new raw materials the less

[1] Materials Policy Commision, vol. V, 1952.

advanced may take up some of the more traditional materials such as cotton, flax and wool, which are no longer so strongly in demand by the richer countries, or they too may move direct from a primitive technique to a highly advanced synthetic process.   The choice between these two methods will depend on the relative costs and returns anticipated.   Whatever choice is made, the world should be able to "support" its increasing population, though not necessarily to give it the standard of life many of its members would like to see established.

CHAPTER III

BRITAIN'S POPULATION

§ 1. *Estimates and Trends.* The 1951 Census count recorded a total population for England and Wales of 43,745 thousand persons,[1] and for Scotland of 5,095 thousand persons.[2] The preceding census took place in 1931. Mid-year estimates of population are made annually by the Registrars-General, and one of the purposes of the Census counts is to check these continuous records; the discrepancy revealed was only 0·2 per cent. The total of 48,840 thousand persons (50·2 million including Northern Ireland) was the highest recorded population since the decennial censuses [3] began to be taken in 1801.

From 1801 to 1841 the decennial rate of increase of the population of England and Wales varied between 14 and 18 per cent; the average decennial rate from 1801 to 1841 was 15·5 per cent. The rate varied over the decades from 1841 to 1911 between 11 and 14 per cent and on a logarithmic graph a straight line indicates a fairly continuous advance slightly reduced after 1841 (Diagram II). But in 1911 there was a second, and much more marked, point of inflexion. The rate of nearly 11 per cent (1901–11) fell to 4·50 and 4·78 per cent for the decades 1931–41 and 1941–51.

[1] *Census 1951, England and Wales, Preliminary Report,* H.M.S.O., 1951, p. x.
[2] *Preliminary Report on the Fifteenth Census of Scotland,* H.M.S.O., Edinburgh, 1951, p. v.
[3] The series is broken by the omission of the census in the war year of 1941.

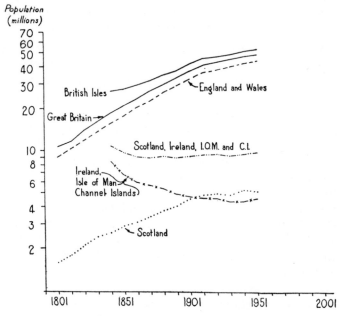

Diagram II.　150 YEARS POPULATION CHANGE, BRITISH ISLES

Source: Table VII, *Census 1951, England & Wales, Preliminary Report.*

The Registrar-General remarked of this series that [1]:

"The important features of the series . . . which cannot be too strongly stressed at the present time, having regard to the frequency of statements concerning the onset of stationary or declining conditions, are that the population continues to grow, that there has been little change in its successive rates of increase for the past forty years, and that so far there is no sign of any tapering away of the successive increments such as

[1] *Census 1951, England and Wales, Preliminary Report,* p. xi.

would normally be expected to herald the early approach of an ultimate population maximum."

Some demographers might well quarrel with this use of the word "normally", since the niceties of their mathematics are designed precisely to reveal trends concealed by movements in the total figures. The Registrar-General's duty is to record facts, however, and to be guided mainly by those facts; refinements imply further assumptions. With regard to England and Wales the facts are indeed very striking, and if the trend were to continue in a slightly modified form,[1] those countries together would have a total of 45·7 million persons in 1961, 47·8 in 1971 and nearly 50 million in 1981, or, say, 56 million for Great Britain. This projection represents a greater percentage increase than any suggested for Great Britain as a whole by demographers or official committees, who have usually tended to extrapolate the falling birth-rate, and to assume that the effect of net migration will be neutral or slight or unfavourable. Two only of the sixteen interesting projections worked out in the Royal Commission's selected papers [2] allowed for net inward migration (only of some 100,000 persons in all). Several of the Royal Commission's projections assumed the fertility of 1935–38, and all have used a constant or declining mortality. On the basis of their various assumptions, the Royal Commission arrived at a total population for Great Britain in 1982 ranging from 46 million to 55 million, and in 2002 (on the same assumptions) from 41 million to 57 million. The point is that a steady rise of 4½ per cent per decade gives a result outside the range of those projections which the Royal Commission seemed to think worthy of detailed discussion.

---

[1] E.g., a decennial increase of 4½ per cent.
[2] Selected papers, Vol. II, 1950, p. 213 ff.

It does not follow, however, that the projection is absurd or unlikely. The population for England and Wales has advanced at a different rate from that of Scotland, or that of the rest of the "British Islands", in which are included the whole of Ireland, the Isle of Man and the Channel Islands. The population of this remainder (i.e., the total excluding England and Wales) has remained practically stable since 1851, going down slightly in economically unfavourable decades and up slightly in others. This apparent stability, however, conceals the different trends in Scotland and the rest of the British Islands (principally Ireland).[1] Scotland alone of these units increased until 1911. Thus, populations in Scotland, Wales (and Monmouthshire), Northern Ireland, the Isle of Man, and the Irish Republic all declined between 1921 and 1931, for example, so that in that decade, while the population for England alone rose by 6·0 per cent, that for the U.K. plus the islands and the Irish Republic (called for convenience the British Islands) rose by only 3·9 per cent. However, the Registrar-General's remark on the smooth growth of the population curve is equally applicable to the total population of these "islands of the British seas" simply because England and Wales is numerically the most important part of the total. If the same simple projection were made to the "islands of the British seas" as to England and Wales it would appear that the 53 millions of 1951 might increase to some 56 millions in 1961, 58 millions in 1971, and so on for some decades. This projection is less likely to be realized than the first, since the stability in the growth of England and Wales was paralleled in the rest of the area by a stability not of growth but of total population; simple projections are of less plausibility, as the rate of development of the

[1] See Diagram II, p. 55.

outer areas of the group might more easily vary from their past rates in either direction, up or down.

During the decade 1921–31 there was a net migration from Scotland of 392,000 persons, and even during the twenty years from 1931–51 Scotland lost some 220,000 persons net by migration. Similarly, Ireland has persistently lost population by migration, especially to England and Wales. These countries gained no less than 525,000 net by immigration from 1931 to 1939, of whom a substantial proportion came from Ireland.

Since 1945 net migration into England and Wales has apparently revived. For the whole period 1939–51 there would, indeed, appear from one Census table to have been a net loss by "migration" of some 20,000,[1] but this particular census table includes war deaths occurring outside the country under the heading "loss by migration". When allowance has been made for war deaths, it appears that there was a net inflow of migrants into England and Wales of 220,000 in the period 1939–51 (745,000 in all from 1931 to 1951).[2] Net migration of 745,000 covering all forces affecting the size of population other than birth and death, can be compared with a "natural increase" (i.e., excess of births over deaths [3]) of 3,048 thousand over twenty years, and works out at nearly 20 per cent of total net increase. Because net migration represents a small figure in relation to *births* the fact that it has been a substantial fraction of the total net increase in England and Wales is often overlooked.

Predictions of the future of migration are naturally very hazardous; in any case, its volume and direction will depend partly upon governmental policy, both in this

[1] *Census 1951, England and Wales Preliminary Report*, Table C, p. xv.
[2] *Ibid.*, p. xiii.
[3] Including war casualties.

country and in those countries to which our emigrants go and from which our immigrants come. But are there not some rather deep underlying economic factors which will help to determine the lines that policy is likely to follow?

There are still a number of overseas countries which hope to benefit economically by the influx of British emigrants, provided that these arrive at a rate at which they can be comfortably absorbed. Details may be left aside at this stage of the discussion. The point, here, is that some emigration is likely to continue for at least the next twenty-five years.

On the other hand, there seems to be no good reason for supposing that those economic factors which resulted in so heavy a net inward migration into England and Wales have yet exhausted themselves; for they were the very factors which are obscurely working to produce the same surface symptoms the world over—rapid growth of urban centres, industrialization, accompanied by de-population first of the less urban areas and finally of the city centres themselves. The phenomenon was systemati-cally treated by Weber in the 1890's although it had been the subject of statisticians' debates at an earlier date.[1] It has continued at an accelerating rate ever since, and shows no sign of losing its momentum. The influx of population into England and Wales was part of a general rearrangement of population within these islands, taking place at the same time as a rapid general increase.

The Report of the Royal Commission [2] was very cautious on the subject of migration. It argued that "there is even less question here than elsewhere of choosing a single assumption as representing the likely course of development". It mentioned the fact that the

---

[1] More particularly in the 1880's.
[2] Cmd. 7695, 1949, par. 231.

balance of net migration for Great Britain was "usually outward" in the last century (i.e., 1847–1948) although inward after 1931. The Report concludes that "it seems safe to say that emigration has so far predominated", statistically, that is, and setting off the inward movement of recent years against the net emigration of the previous century or so.

If it is considered that the real national income of Great Britain may, despite the difficulties of overseas trade, rise slightly, then continued industrialization and urbanization of the country may be assumed. The precise form of that development is indeed very uncertain, nor is it predictable in exactly which places the greatest increases will take place. But that there will be a continued growth of certain types of town and of some of the conurbations (to be described presently) is more likely than not. From this assumption net migration into England and Wales seems practically certain; whether or not there must be net migration into Great Britain or the "British Islands" depends upon how far the rest of that area continues to provide an excess population for England and Wales.

The Registrar-General's optimism applies not only to migration but to the birth-rate; the Commission's Report was, on the other hand, professionally pessimistic on this subject. On this point the Report so far committed itself as to conclude: [1]

"One future development . . . we *can* forecast with a good deal of confidence, namely, a substantial decline in the annual number of births over the next 15 years."

Estimating the figures in 1948, the Report's authors guessed that average annual births for the period 1947–52

[1] *Ibid.*, par. 201.

in Great Britain would amount to 804,000. The recorded total has in fact been 836,000, so that their figure was some 4 per cent too low.

The basis of their projections was their belief in the stability of the size of the family. As they put it,[1] "it is clear that the size of the family will be decisive for the future number of births in Great Britain". The reverse is also true, since the future number of births will be decisive for the size of the family. The Royal Commission were not, however, indulging in an empty truism, since their point was that the important variable nowadays was the size of family determined upon by the average married couple. Thus, on their view, the number of births in any one year, or group of years, might be misleading if it was due not to a change in the intentions of married couples but only to the fact that marriages had been taking place at an earlier age.

The Royal Commission gave a useful rule of thumb to assist speculation on this difficult topic: the figure of 700,000 births annually for Great Britain. If the annual number of births remains greater than this figure, the total population will continue to show some net natural increase; at about this figure, stability of population will gradually be established; below it, a decline would eventually set in. Up to 1952 the decline had not yet resulted in births below the critical figure.

But the question still remains how far "average size of family" is itself a variable that is going to remain stable, and evidence that it has been stable in the recent past is not necessarily conclusive, or even very relevant. Social habits have changed quite rapidly in some recent decades in many countries. It is necessary to find the principal variables which will determine size of family—or, more

[1] *Ibid.*, par. 207.

directly, the total number of births each year—in the future. Arithmetic is only incidental to any prediction. In any case the size of "completed families" can only be known some decades after marriage.

The factors that are going to affect the total number of births in future are innumerable, but some of the principal ones are undoubtedly economic. Others are such specific factors as the availability of particular resources, and others again are social factors such as emulation, fashion and family attitudes generally. In trying to guess how all these are going to work out, it is well to remember for how short a time certain social changes have been accepted, for example a national health service, the social goal of full employment, school meals and special milk for children, family allowances and so on. The experiment of living in a world of full employment has not long been tried; as for living in a world of general economic security, the experiment has yet to be made.

Two objections have been made to the view that improved economic conditions would slow down the fall in the annual number of births; the first is that, on the contrary, the differences in the birth-rates of the higher and lower (i.e., richer and poorer) social classes in the past indicate that economic advancement makes for a limitation of size of families, and the second objection is that such correlation between economic change and birth-rates as can be observed in the past has been of short duration (in the main, cyclical) and therefore of little importance in relation to a long-term downward trend.

The first of these objections may be met in two ways: observation suggests that the differential birth-rates of the different social classes has been modified in recent years.[1]

[1] See "Family Anatomy", *The Economist*, 22 November 1952, p. 520 (article based on the second volume of the sample report of the 1951 Census for Great Britain).

Secondly, in a more equal society, with certain social services fully maintained and domestic life thus more firmly established on a workable basis, a slight improvement in the standard of life might well be expected *a priori* to result in rather larger instead of rather smaller families. The past is very little guide as to whether this would be so or not. The rewards of social advancement have tended often to be taken in various forms of display expenditure, but in a social system where these were discouraged a different reaction might be more common. Economic encouragement of a specific kind for large families might assist this process.

Special conditions of the past may, too, account for the apparently short-term correlation between the birth-rate and economic prosperity. To assume that rising standards of life necessarily imply smaller families is to project past experience into a future in which social relationships may have very profoundly changed.

It seems unfortunate to have to remain agnostic on this important issue, but at this stage of the argument the most that can be said is that a rise in the number of births is almost as likely as a continuing fall, and that a long-term positive correlation between real national income and size of family may quite possibly, with a suitable social background, establish itself. The future growth of the population, on this view, is to be determined by (as well as partly determining) the rate of material progress of the economy as a whole.

§ 2. *Urbanization.* Cities grow in two ways, by natural increase and by immigration; and in two senses, by an increase of numbers and by the extension of their boundaries. The economic and social boundaries often advance more rapidly than the corresponding administrative extensions, so that, for a growing "conurbation", the urbanized district extends over a wider area as time goes on, although administrative changes often lag behind the fact itself.

Exact statistical measurement of the growth of urbanization is for these reasons very often impossible. At any given moment a boundary is arbitrary, since people beyond the boundary have some economic links in their daily lives with those within it, and the boundary, however defined, ought sometimes to be re-drawn. Yet the spread of cities has been as important a change as the fluctuations of their own populations.

The effect of the extension of a city's influence in the later stages is seen in the form of a depopulation of the central districts (a decline in the numbers of those who sleep there, that is; the day-time population may remain stable or even rise) ; although, of course, this same depopulation may also be the symptom of a general decline.

Some indication of how these movements work out in Great Britain may be discovered in the census figures for the principal conurbations. There are six such conurbations officially listed for England and Wales, and their population as a whole rose from 1931 to 1951, though more slowly than the population of the whole country (by 3·1 against 9·5 per cent for England and Wales). If each of the conurbations is divided into an inner and outer ring, the inner rings lost no less than 11·5 per cent of their population in twenty years, while the outer rings (including their smaller urban areas) gained 21·2 per cent. By 1951, indeed, the population in the outer rings of the conurbations (8,900,000) exceeded that in the central areas (8,000,000), nor is there any reason for supposing that the process is at an end.

Much has been made of the social disadvantages of

conurbation, such as congestion of traffic, bad atmosphere, poor living conditions due to overcrowding, the
creation of "bhghted" inner areas as the town expands
outwards, and of distress in other parts of the country if
all new industry is attracted elsewhere.   All these evils
require remedy, but they are not in themselves evils
arising from general over-population.   Some of them arise
from failure to adjust the social capital of a central urban
area to its new functions, as the built-up area which it
regularly serves becomes more densely inhabited, and
indeed physically wider.   The remedy for this must be
sought (and is being sought) in re-planning.   But despite
the need for quite elaborate control and prompting by
government authorities to promote the correct changes,
and to mitigate their incidental hardships, it cannot be
soundly argued that the growth of urban civilization is
in itself a tide that ought to be dammed or rolled back,
by the British any more than by any other government.

This is a similar conclusion to that of Professor Dennison
in his well-known minority report to the Scott Committee,[1]
when he looked at the obverse side of the same coin—
the alleged loss of amenity accruing as a result of the
decline in the agricultural population ; he looked to "more
effective planning" for a remedy rather than to a new
set of "principles", always provided that (town and
country planning) control was not restrictive or inelastic.
His main thesis was that the economic welfare criterion
should not be left out of account : "It is clearly desirable
that the people should have as high a material standard
of life as possible." [2]

The difficulty remains of how to assess the non-
economic criteria, the relative advantages of different

[1] Cmd. 6378, 1942, pp. 100–123.
[2] *Ibid.*, p. 120, par. 67.

"ways of life", for example city *versus* rural life from the point of view of culture or social development. Much depends not only on subjective judgment on these matters but on the objective conditions in which the different ways of life are to flourish. If the growing urban areas are inadequately drained, lighted and policed, as in some manufacturing towns of England in the early stages of the industrial revolution, the social price paid for moving from the country to the town may be high. If a well-planned modern city is compared with a well-planned and prosperous rural area the relative advantages are not so clear. The growth of garden suburbs, and of "commuting" to dormitory villages, suggests that many people, given a choice, prefer to live in rural or semi-rural conditions, even at the cost of some material disadvantages, such as the cost of fares and the wear and tear of travelling.

A specialized literature has been created by protagonists of different views as to what the "city of the future" should be like, and views range from those who want to see modern civilization build round the indefinite extension of the garden suburb idea, so that towns are ultimately dispersed more widely, the siting of shopping centres, etc., being related to the assumption that every family is to own its car or cars, to those who want multi-storey dwellings erected on the outskirts, or even in the centre, of existing urban conglomerations.

§ 3. *Age and Sex Distribution.* In the Census count of persons in Great Britain in 1951 there were 25·4 million females and 23·4 million males, a "surplus" of 2 million females due to the exclusion of the armed forces overseas from the count, to the superior chances of life of females and to historical causes such as two world wars contribu-

ting to further excess than would otherwise have existed.
Over the country as a whole there were 109 females for
every 100 males at that time.

But, as is usual in urbanized countries, there was a
greater percentage excess of females in the urban than
in the rural areas. In the conurbations there were 112
females to every 100 males, and in other cities of 100,000
inhabitants or more the proportion was 111:100. The
concentration of women in the urban areas applied
to all age groups, though much more to the oldest than
to the youngest group. In the two most active age
groups, (a) 15–19 and (b) 20–64, the excess was for (a)
very marked and for (b) just noticeable. In the 15–19
group, for example, the national ratio was 105, while in
the conurbations it was 118, in the next group of cities
125. In the rural areas, where males were in excess, the
figure was as low as 74 women per 100 men for this age-
group. Females aged 20–64 lived in conurbations in the
ratio of 111 to 100 males, and in the rural areas in a ratio
of about 100 to 100.

If a comparison is made between the birth-rates of the
great conurbations and other urban areas of England and
Wales, and the rural areas—both being divided further
to show the Northern and North-Western Regions
separately from the rest of the country—it will be seen
that the North and North-Western cities have a crude
birth-rate that exceeds the average (by 7 per cent in this
case). The other groups had birth-rates a few per cent
less than the average for the country, which has been
equated with 100. To generalize: the northern towns-
man's proclivity to have children offsets the declined
families of the country people everywhere, and of the
cities and towns in the midlands, the east and the south.

One reason for the crude birth-rate in the rural areas

being below the average is that there are, on the whole, fewer women of child-bearing age (say 15–49) than marriageable men (say 15–64) in the country districts; as column three of Table VIII shows, there were only 89 women (of these ages) to 100 men (of these ages) in the rural districts all over the country. The "refined" rate referred to in the table divides total births by numbers of women in the age-group 15–49. This "refined birth-rate" was 7 per cent greater in "southern" rural areas, and 3 per cent in northern, than the national average ("southern" here referring to England and Wales apart from the Northern and North-Western regions).

This table brings out several other points of interest. If "refined birth-rate" is plotted against "female/male ratio" for England and Wales exclusive of the northern regions there would be three points:

Conurbations	92 : 105
Other urban areas	100 : 101
Rural areas	107 : 89

giving an apparent negative relationship. The districts with higher female/male ratios have a relatively low birth-rate. The cities attract women into employment rather than into marriage and motherhood; the country districts have a low proportion of females to males, but a relatively higher birth-rate.

The figures for the northern districts follow a distinctly different pattern, apparently because of the relatively higher birth-rates in the conurbations of the north-west and north-east, a differential due perhaps to social and religious differences.

Such analyses as these suggest that projections of future population change, even in terms of natural increase, must imply, or be based upon, assumptions as to the social

Table VIII.—COMPARISONS BETWEEN THE BIRTH-RATE AND THE
FEMALE/MALE RATIO FOR SELECTED AREAS IN ENGLAND
AND WALES.

(Index numbers: Average for England and Wales = 100)

| | Birth-rates expressed as Index numbers | | Female/Male Ratio (Females 15–49/ Males 15–64) |
	Crude Birth-rate (Births per 1,000 of Total Population)	Refined Birth-rate (Births per 1,000 of Females Age 15–49)	
England and Wales (excluding Northern and North-Western Regions):			
Conurbations . .	96 ⎫ 98	92 ⎫ 96	105 ⎫ 103
Other urban areas .	101 ⎭	100 ⎭	101 ⎭
Rural areas . .	99	107	89
Northern and North-Western Regions			
Conurbations . .	109 ⎫ 107	108 ⎫ 107	103 ⎫ 102
Other urban areas .	104 ⎭	105 ⎭	100 ⎭
Rural areas . .	98	103	89
London and South-Eastern England . . .	93	89	107
Remainder of England and Wales	103	104	98

Sources: Births from *Registrar-General's Statistical Review*, 1950.
Population data from *Census of Great Britain 1951; One per cent
Sample Tables*.

patterns of future living.   It is evident from any study
of the nineteenth century that the distribution of the
female population throughout the country was profoundly
affected by the changing economic demand for different
types of female labour.   In the twentieth century, not
least in the decade of the 1940's, there were further substantial modifications in these employment opportunities.

The further reduction in domestic service, and the war-time employment and mobilization of women, affected their geographical distribution, their marriage opportunities and their social attitudes; and it would be extremely rash to predict, or to imply by a projection, that further changes in these factors will not take place.

The birth-rates of the towns, and especially of the outer rings of the conurbations, encourage the presumption that urbanized populations are capable of reproducing themselves by natural increase, although their present and future numbers are, and will be, partly determined by net immigration.

The power of population, that is the numbers of potential parents (adults physically capable of reproduction), does not seem to have been gravely impaired in Great Britain, nor likely to decline below a critical level for some time to come. If any series is considered which shows the curve of numbers of females coming into the child-bearing age-group, this fact becomes clear, especially if falling mortality rates and improved chances of life are considered too. This does not mean that the number of births will necessarily rise, or remain above the level of 700,000 annually for many more years. All that can be reasonably well established is that the power of population, in the sense defined, still exists.

§ 4. *Distribution by Occupations.* The main changes in the proportions of the occupied population in the forty years from 1911 to 1951 are summarized in Table IX. The "occupied" population included children as young as 10 years in 1911, but no younger than 15 in 1951; the total rose by 20 per cent for males and 27 per cent for females over this period. Among males the percentage of those occupied in agriculture or fishing fell from 10 to

6 per cent, in mining and quarrying from 10 to 5 per cent, in textiles from 5 to 3 per cent, and in personal service from 2 to 1 per cent. The percentage employed in the distributive trades is also thought to have fallen, but the figures are estimates only. The metals and vehicles occupations, chemicals, building, contracting, public administration and the professions all showed increases. For females most emphasis must be placed upon the heavy percentage declines in personal service, textiles and clothing, on the proportionate rises in the importance of metals, engineering and vehicles, the distributive trades, and the professions. The figures summarize a chapter of social history: the decline of the female servant class, the decline of the textile and clothing industries relatively to other occupations, and the rise of the shop assistant, the female industrial employee and the office worker or professional woman—these changes have been identified with the progressive political and social emancipation of women although it would be a gross over-simplification to suppose that the one change implied the other.

Thus in 1911 women's employment was concentrated in four groups (textiles, clothing and the various kinds of service adding to 69 per cent of the total), but by 1951 these accounted for only 34 per cent of the total occupied females.

According to the Family Census of 1946 the average size of family of professional and administrative workers in Great Britain was about 1·6, while that of unskilled labourers was at least twice as large.[1] A fertility enquiry also reported by the Royal Commission showed that for a certain group of marriages between 1920 and 1934 non-manual workers with "higher" education (above elementary school standard) had smaller families than those who

[1] Cmd. 7695, par. 408, p. 152.

Table IX.—Analysis of the Occupied Population in England and Wales by Industry Groups.

(Per cent of total occupied in each case)

Industry Group	Males 1911 10 and over	Males 1921 12 and over	Males 1931 14 and over	Males 1951 15 and over	Females 1911 10 and over	Females 1921 12 and over	Females 1931 14 and over	Females 1951 15 and over
1. Agriculture and fishing	10	9	8	6	2	2	1	2
2. Mining and quarrying	10	11	8	5	*	*	*	*
3. Non-metalliferous metals	1	2	2	2	1	1	1	1
4. Chemicals, etc.	1	1	1	2	1	1	1	1
5. Metals, engineering, vehicles	12	16	13	21	2	5	4	8
6. Textiles	5	4	4	3	14	13	11	8
7. Leather goods	1	1	*	*	*	*	*	*
8. Clothing	3	3	3	2	15	10	10	7
9. Food and drink	3	3	3	3	3	4	4	4
10. Wood and cork manufactures	2	2	2	2	1	1	*	1
11. Paper, printing	2	2	2	2	2	2	3	3
12. Other manufactures	1	1	1	1	1	1	*	2
13. Building and contracting	7	6	8	9	*	*	*	1
14. Transport	10	10	11	10	*	1	2	3
15. Distributive trades	14†	13†	14	10	7†	15†	15	17
16. Insurance, finance	3†	1†	2	2	*	*	1	2
17. Public administration and defence	6	8	7	10	4	7	3	4
18. Professions	3	2	4	4	7	7	9	10
19. Personal Service	2	2	2	1	26	20	22	13
20. Other services	4†	4†	5	5	14†	10†	11	13
	100%	100%	100%	100%	100%	100%	100%	100%
Occupied population	11·5 mn.			13·8 mn.	4·8 mn.			6·1 mn.
Index of increase (In occupied labour force; aged 15 and over in 1951, but 10 and over in 1911; 1911 = 100.)	100			120	100			127

Source: Relevant Census statistics. N.B. The figures for the four dates are not completely comparable owing to changes in method of classification and in the various age limits.   † Estimated.   * Less than 1 per cent.

had had less education, and similarly for manual workers (who had larger families than non-manual in both categories).[1] These, and similar facts, have long been observed and recorded, and have given rise to doubts as to the future quality of the British population. The main fear that has been expressed is that, although social differences in fertility may narrow, they will still remain, and that the consequence will be the over-breeding of persons with less successful social characteristics (less successful in every respect, that is, but that of the biological act of breeding itself), and that hence there will be a relative decrease in each generation in the numbers of those likely to inherit qualities which lead to social success and esteem.

One such quality is sometimes held to be "intelligence", an abstract quality which is believed to be partly hereditary and partly subject to environment (that is, susceptible of being hidden by adverse educational influences). The argument is then re-stated as follows. On the whole, according to intelligence tests taken at schools, children of greater intelligence come on average from smaller families than the less intelligent. Since, by this hypothesis, intelligence is partly a hereditary characteristic, each succeeding generation of children will tend to be, on average, less intelligent. Each generation the general level of innate intelligence of the nation is bound to decline. This is an alarming proposition, which has been supported by many distinguished scientists, and not merely by historians theorizing about the "decline of the West", and it deserves very serious attention.

Many tests seem to have established the general proposition that, on average, the less intelligent children have belonged to the larger families in British schools where

[1] *Ibid.*, par. 410.

varying tests have been applied since before World War I. What the tests have failed to show is that the average intelligence of schoolchildren is declining. The question is what interpretation to put on these facts.

The first point to observe is that the actual predictions made by the early enthusiasts for the technique of intelligence tests have not in fact been fulfilled. They predicted unequivocally that the intelligence of the nation would fall, and, according to their own techniques (incidentally modified considerably over the years), this verifiable fall has not taken place. While it may still be true that *innate* intelligence is falling (if there is a scientific basis for the distinction between "innate" and "total" intelligence) observed total intelligence, as evidenced by behaviour in intelligence tests, shows no corresponding decline.

The argument that intelligence is mainly hereditary seems closely analogous to the similar argument that bodily stature is also a mainly hereditary characteristic. A school of thought exists which questions the validity of the statistical methods used in many of the so-called "proofs" of the hereditary influence.[1]

In the standard statistical textbooks tables are often given of the heights of fathers and sons, and second degree statistics (e.g., correlation coefficients) are used to demonstrate the hereditary influence. But a first degree statistic, average height, for example, is often neglected, although this may be compatible less with a hereditary theory than with the simpler theory that improved diet and environment improve stature. Both influences are undoubtedly at work; what is fallacious is to ignore the lesson of first

[1] See Barnet Woolf, 1952. I am indebted to Professor 'Espinasse for calling my attention to this, and the subsequent reference in this chapter.

order statistics showing increasing stature with each generation.   Similarly of intelligence.

In about thirty years the average intelligence of Scottish schoolchildren rose by about twice as much as it was expected to fall according to the genetical theory.   These results some writers have attempted to explain away as due to the better practice at intelligence tests alleged, or supposed, to be indulged in by modern schoolchildren, but this argument tacitly admits the factor of environment as being of importance; and environment correlates with home conditions, which are affected by size of family income.   There seems little reason for the plain man to doubt that level of income and environment raises the standard in the community both of intelligence and of bodily stature.

An *a priori* argument of Professor Penrose [1] may also be considered; if a hypothetical population is divided into three groups in respect of intelligence, say I.Q.103 for the best, comprising 90 per cent of the fertile population, a small group with I.Q.73 comprising 10 per cent of the population, which is more fertile than the first group, and a fractional third group with very low intelligence and low fertility as well, and the extreme assumption is adopted that intelligence is due to a single perfectly additive pair of genes called A and a, the upper group will be all AA, the small inferior group Aa, and the weaklings aa.

On the assumption of two types of mating only, $AA \times AA$ will produce nothing but slightly superior offspring.   In the inferior group $Aa \times Aa$ will, on orthodox genetic theory, produce $\frac{1}{4}AA$, $\frac{1}{2}Aa$ and $\frac{1}{4}aa$.   It can be calculated that this population will be in perfect equilibrium in respect to the (assumed inherited) characteristic,

[1] Penrose, 1949, p. 124.

intelligence, *if* the birth-rate of the inferior group is rather more than twice that of the superior group. Thus a considerably higher birth-rate is required to prevent the inferior group from gradually dying out. The particular result follows, of course, from the figures chosen by Professor Penrose for his example, but the result is instructive.

The general argument follows from the assumption that a fraction of the reproduced offspring of the "mixed" group (*Aa*'s mating with *Aa*'s) turn out to be sub-lethal *aa*'s, incapable of survival. On the other hand, another proportion of the same mixed group's offspring replenish the ranks of the *AA*'s who would otherwise tend to diminish in proportion of total population because of their own lower birth-rate. Furthermore, it may well be, for all that we can easily state, that some societies, and particularly modern industrial societies, require for their operation a large mass (or a small mass—in either case a pre-determined proportion) of only averagely endowed individuals. This will evidently be the case when the techniques of production absolutely require fairly large numbers of unskilled, or only semi-skilled, workers.

The differential class birth-rates observed in our societies may then be, in part at least, the consequence of social pressures tending to lead at least partially to the "correct" numbers of individuals being born of given grades of intelligence. Of course, it would be absurd to pretend that the adjustment of labour supply to demand can be exact in the long-run, that is, over the long period of years required to raise and educate a family. But if demand for trained skilled "labour", right up to the top professional and managerial grades, is persistently high, the working-class may in favourable conditions react by throwing up a proportion of persons with first-class brains, who can be sent at the expense of some sacrifice by the family to be educated or trained for a higher social class. All this is speculation; the point that has been established by Professor Penrose is that even on the most extreme assumptions as to the importance of genetical influences there can be no *a priori* case established for predicting a general decline in national intelligence. This does not, however, mean that measures, or circumstances, which discourage the more intelligent members of society from reproduction are not deplorable in their effects.

PART II

ANALYSIS

CHAPTER IV

THE MALTHUSIAN THEORY

§ 1. *Malthus as a Publicist.* Thomas Robert Malthus, the second in a family of eight children, was born in 1766. His father, Daniel Malthus, was a country gentleman, with dilettante intellectual interests, who was honoured to receive David Hume and Jean-Jacques Rousseau as guests at his house near Dorking one month after the prodigious Thomas Robert had seen the light. Daniel Malthus admired the eighteenth-century enlightenment, and caused his children to be brought up by private education, sending Thomas Robert in due course to a tutor who prepared him for Cambridge. Robert Malthus entered Jesus College in 1784, took orders in 1788, and became a fellow of his college in 1793, a fellowship which he held until he resigned the post on his marriage in 1804. He accepted a curacy in 1796, and wrote an insignificant political pamphlet, attacking Pitt's Government, in the same year. Two years later, after the celebrated argument (described in the preface to his essay) with his father, who defended Godwin's views set out in *Political Justice* in favour of the possibility of Utopia, T. R. Malthus published the first edition of his *Essay on the Principle of Population as it affects the Future Improvement of Society, with remarks on the speculations of Mr. Godwin, M. Condorcet, and other writers.*[1]

As a publicist, Malthus was enormously successful. He

[1] These biographical facts have been taken from Dr. G. F. McCleary's *The Malthusian Population Theory*, 1953, from which the reader may derive a full, accurate, but wholly favourable view of Malthus's population theories.

set out to attack the poor laws, and he lived to see them repealed. On this subject he converted Pitt, who dropped the New Poor Law Bill of 1800. His first essay was intended to refute Godwin, and Godwin's eclipse was complete.[1] In 1811 Shelley was to hear with "inconceivable emotion" that Godwin was not yet "enrolled in the list of the honourable dead".[2] Other social forces, public and personal, contributed to Godwin's period of oblivion; Coleridge, for example, had ceased to hymn Godwin with any ardent lays, and Southey and Wordsworth were living to regret the naïve optimism with which they had welcomed Godwin's quiet but effective attacks upon superstition and the abuses of the established order of government. Godwin's utopianism, like that of others, though effective in its attack on abuses, and attractive in its confidence in human enlightenment and reason, was open to deadly counter-thrusts in many of its positive propositions, such as the famous views on marriage which were easy for critics both to distort and to deride. Through Shelley himself, and through his earlier influence on Place and Owen, and indeed on generations of radicals, Godwin's influence was perpetuated. But he was doomed to be practically ineffective in his own lifetime, although he outlived Malthus, dying in 1836 in his eightieth year.

Many strands were joined in Godwin's thought, both of rationalist and dissenting ancestry. The principal point which Malthus selected for attack was his belief that human institutions, rather than the intrinsic vices of

[1] As Godwin admitted in the preface to his "Enquiry" of 1820: "the Essay on Population has gotten possession of the public mind." (Godwin, 1820, p. viii). The first edition of his *Enquiry concerning the Principles of Political Justice* was published in 1793, the second in 1796, and the third in 1798.

[2] Rodway, 1952, p. 45. Shelley was not, apparently, ironical in this passage, but had genuinely believed that Godwin was no longer alive.

individual human beings, were the main cause of the evils of mankind; he looked forward to an imaginary period of reforms ending with the dissolution of government—the final "withering away" of the state.[1]

Godwin wrote:

"With what delight must every well-informed friend of mankind look forward, to the auspicious period, the dissolution of political government, of that brute engine, which has been the only perennial cause of the vices of mankind. . . ."

This was the somewhat extreme and flaccid optimism that Malthus discerned in his own father's presuppositions, and which, as a young Cambridge intellectual of some capacity as a mathematician, he set out to deflate and refute.   Malthus wished to show that owing to his "principle of population", vice and misery must always be with mankind, in accordance with the Biblical text about the poor, except, according to the qualification of his second edition, in so far as "moral restraint" was exercised, and in his view it was unlikely to be exercised very extensively.   He succeeded in making his point, and, from his day to this, vice and misery have never been wholly dissociated in the minds of Western civilized persons from high birth-rates among the poor.

As the study by Mr. Kenneth Smith[2] very well shows, almost every logical objection that can be brought against Malthus's arguments was publicly expressed, and often well and trenchantly expressed, by critics such as Hazlitt, Booth, Place, Grahame, Weyland and a host of others,

---

[1] This aspect of Godwin's thought derives perhaps from his own sensitiveness to the brutality of the state's methods in most of the countries of contemporary Europe rather than from any particular literary source.

[2] Smith, 1951.

in Malthus's own lifetime.[1]   Yet it was Malthus's doctrine
that survived to be discussed, and not that of any of his
critics.   The revival of Malthusianism at intervals of
some thirty years (for instance in the periods 1885–93,
1918–25 and 1946–52) is a subject for separate study.
What cannot be denied is that Malthus himself was, on
his chosen ground, a most formidable controversialist.
From what sources came the strength of his position?

Malthus, unlike Ricardo, did not wish to usher in the
new phase of rapid capitalist expansion already heralded
by the earlier technical developments of the industrial
revolution, but rather to defend a society dominated
economically by land-owning and land-holding classes.
In two little discussed pamphlets he warmly defended the
Corn Laws. But his population theory fitted into the
intellectual structure of the Ricardian system very well,
or, at least, it could be adapted to Ricardo's ideas, and
provide the basis for his theory of wages and of profits.
The general thesis that population tended to outrun
subsistence pleased nearly everybody, capitalist apologists
as well as those who defended the landed interest.   One
element in his strength is that all schools of classical
economists adapted his theory to their own ends.   Even
Engels thought that Malthus was "right in his way"
(i.e., with reference to bourgeois society) in asserting that
there are always more people on hand than can be maintained from the available means of subsistence; but of
course he and Marx gave a different explanation from
Malthus for this phenomenon.   But they fully recognized
the importance of the Malthusian theory of population,

[1] Dr. McCleary dismisses Hazlitt in a footnote referring to that great
writer's indiscreet *Liber Amoris* (see McCleary, 1953, p. 101).   That even
modern apologists for Malthus have recourse to such irrelevancy exposes
them to the accusation that they have no better argument to put
forward.

which they thought had been "invented" to reconcile the otherwise inexplicable phenomena of capitalist society.[1]

Malthus's population theory needs, moreover, to be read in relation to the preceding population theories of the eighteenth century; they were many and various.

Cantillon's theory,[2] for example, was elaborate and subtle, and evidently based upon careful observation. He thought of the landowners as the controlling class of society, and of land as "the source whence all wealth is produced". Population growth depended, in the main, upon the subsistence produced at the behest of the landed proprietors, the proportion of this which those proprietors made available for the hire of labour, and the standards of life current among the wage-earning and land-owning classes respectively.

Thus population depends, in Cantillon's view, upon what might now be called the "strategic decisions" taken by the landed proprietors. If the proprietors live far from their land "Horses must be fed for the transport into the city", and "the more Horses there are in a state the less food will remain for the People". The number of inhabitants in a state depended chiefly upon the means allotted to them for their support, and the amount of these means in turn depended chiefly on the "Taste, Humours and Manner of Living of the Proprietors of Land".

He thought, further, that the population of a country would tend to be increased or diminished as a result of

[1] When pressed to answer whether over-population could arise under communism Engels admitted "the abstract possibility" of a necessity to impose limits on numbers, but added that if regulation of numbers ever became necessary only a communist society could carry out such regulation successfully. (See the letter to Kautsky, quoted in Meek, 1953, p. 108.) Some occasions for testing the correctness of this opinion may occur if communist societies survive.
[2] Cantillon, 1755 (reprinted 1931).

international trade, according to the degree to which that trade resulted in a net import of necessaries. For example, the import of Brussels lace into France would tend to diminish the French population if wine were exported to buy the lace, since the wine would cost France the use of many thousands of acres.

Cantillon thus linked the size of the population with the amount of food and necessaries available, as Malthus did in a much blunter form with his first postulate (that food was necessary to man). But he had no conviction that Malthus's second postulate on the geometrical ratio of population increase operated unrestrainedly—or, putting the matter another way, he fully understood as a result of observation the phenomenon described by Malthus as "moral restraint".[1]

Quesnay and the Physiocrats also believed that population tends to grow as the supply of subsistence expands, and they, in their turn, began to concern themselves with the procreative instincts of man which, they feared, resulted in a downward pressure on wages. But they seemed, on the whole, to think that such downward pressure was self-adjusting, since the excessive misery temporarily engendered would lead to a reduction of population by emigration and a fall in the number of births. As agriculture became more prosperous, on the other hand, real wages might rise above a mere subsistence level, and the tendency towards over-procreation was by no means an inexorable law.[2]

These schools of French writers failed to anticipate

---

[1] If there were not sufficient necessaries, Cantillon thought "the People will diminish in number. Some will be forced to leave the country for lack of employment; others, not seeing the necessary means of raising children, will not marry or will marry late ..." (Spengler, 1942, p. 116).

[2] Spengler, pp. 208-9.

Malthus, except in the very general sense of discussing fully the relation of population to food supplies, and the dangers of too great a rate of procreation.

Thus on *two* essential points Malthus's views were diametrically different from those of many earlier writers. On the first point he was opposed to Wallace, one of the British writers who most closely foreshadowed some of his arguments.[1] Malthus clearly owed very much to Wallace's exposition.[2] But there was this important point of difference, that Wallace, like his French contemporaries, thought that any evil day of over-population lay ahead at some unpredictable date in the future, whereas Malthus often insisted that it had already arrived.

On the second point, too, Malthus's theory was sharply different from that of any of his predecessors. They were willing to discuss the "defects of government" in Wallace's phrase, or the shortcomings of absolutism in France, as obstacles to a greater population; in other words, to treat human institutions, like the state, as variables that could be changed to meet changing social needs. Malthus was concerned to point out a "principle of population" which was, in his view, immutable and inexorable, and which rendered most proposed "improvements" of social

---

[1] Wallace had written in 1753: "Indeed had it not been for the errors and the vices of mankind, and for the defects of government and of education, the earth must have been much better peopled, perhaps might have been overstocked, many ages ago; and as these causes operate more or less strongly, the earth will be better or worse peopled at different times." He had added in 1761, that: "Under a perfect government, the inconveniences of having a family would be so entirely removed, children would be so well taken care of, and every thing become so favourable to populousness, that though some sickly seasons or dreadful plagues in particular climates might cut off multitudes, yet in general, mankind would increase so prodigiously, that the earth would at last be overstocked, and become unable to support its numerous inhabitants."

[2] Wallace wrote clearly of the forces making for a reduction of any surplus population that there was "no need of miracles for this purpose. The vices of mankind are sufficient."

institutions valueless and nugatory. The deeper significance of his position as a publicist is well explained by
Dr. Spengler, who points out that Malthus's predecessors
were, on the other hand, chiefly concerned with the
discovery (and diffusion) of means to dissolve the evils
of political absolutism.

Malthus took up the defence of property and of (to a
large extent) the social *status quo* at the very moment
that technological progress was making itself felt. Increased opportunities for the growth of incomes seemed
to be about to occur; real wages could then rise, and
many established relationships would become obsolete,
and disappear with or without some violent social upheaval. Malthus was essentially a lover of a well-ordered
society, stable and beneficent, and governed by recognized religious principles. Some kinds of progress there
might be, but any advance in living standards must be,
he hoped—and he believed that he had discovered that it
would be—associated with the exercise of moral courage
and restraint. The task of governments was to protect
property and prevent its abuse, to discourage pauperism
by abolishing such expedients as the Speenhamland
system, and in every way possible to link real incomes
with effort and work, treating idleness as a social crime.

§ 2. *Malthus's Postulates and Arguments.* Malthus's principle, in its deductive form, was derived from two postulates and one assumption. The postulates were that food
was necessary for the existence of man, and that sexual
passion was a determined and unchanging force sufficiently
strong to maintain some geometrical rate of population
increase. The assumption was that the production of
food could be increased only in the ratio 1, 2, 3, 4, 5, 6,
7, 8, 9, that is in an arithmetical ratio, at the same time

as population tended to increase, or had the "power" to increase, in the geometrical ratio 1, 2, 4, 8, 16, 32, 64, 128, 256 and so on.

The assumption of the arithmetical increase in food was subject to the qualification that "fresh starts" in agriculture, that is improvements due to reorganization or the introduction of new techniques, could from time to time raise the level from which the increase began.

Reasoning from the postulates and the assumption Malthus concluded that, unless marriages were postponed, or restraint on reproduction otherwise introduced, population would always tend to outrun food supply; hence some "checks" would be imposed by "nature", or as we should perhaps say, would arise from the situation itself. These checks could in general be described as "vice and misery".   In the second edition the possibility of "moral restraint" was admitted, by which term Malthus meant the kind of prudence with regard to marriage more clearly and objectively described by Cantillon.

As Edwin Cannan shrewdly remarked:

> "The soundest economists will hesitate if asked directly, 'What is the principle of population as understood by Malthus?'" [1]

Cannan answered his own question with the statement that:

> ". . . It seems probable, it would be rash to say more, that in the first edition of the *Essay* 'the principle of population' is that the growth of population must necessarily be checked by misery or prudential motives."

Certainly there can be no doubt of the position adopted

[1] Cannan, 1924, p. 134.

in the first *Essay*, as this was purely deductive. The argument in the *Encyclopædia Britannica* of 1824 [1] was fundamentally unchanged. From the two postulates as set out in the first edition verbatim which were:

"that food is necessary to the existence of man"

and

"that the passion between the sexes is necessary, and will remain nearly in its present state"[2],

Malthus argued that "the power of population is indefinitely greater than the power in the earth to produce subsistence for man." The jump in the argument from the postulates to the conclusion depends, of course, upon the assumption. In the next paragraph the assumption is stated:

"Population, when unchecked, increases in a geometrical ratio. A slight acquaintance with numbers will show the immensity of the first power in comparison with the second . . ."

The postulates and the assumption may fairly be identified as Malthus's major contribution to the subject, [3] and if Malthus was wrong either one or both of the postulates must be rejected, and/or the assumption about the ratios. The later editions of the *Essay* "explained" his position, however, with many qualifications.

But before turning to the *qualified* theory it may be worth while first to explain the merits of the earlier

[1] Malthus, 1824.

[2] Modern apologists for Malthus sum up his principle as being that it is "easier" for mankind to produce children than to produce subsistence (see McCleary, 1953, p. 157). But precisely what does "easier" mean in this context? And, however defined, can such a statement be universally valid?

[3] Sir James Steuart, in his *Inquiry* of 1767, had fully explained the relation of populations, both human and animal, to food supply (Vol. 1, Book I, chap. 3).

deductive statement and secondly to examine reasons
for supposing it to be false.

Malthus argued that, because of his postulates, there
must be "a strong and constantly operating check on
population from the difficulty of subsistence". Ignoring
for the moment the social implication of this statement
(which Malthus at once stated—"this difficulty . . . must
necessarily be felt by a large portion of mankind"), its
brilliance as a wide generalization needs to be observed ;
for at one blow Malthus placed mankind on the same level
as the other species of creation. He put man in relation
to the restraints of his environment, and it was this aspect
of his work that supplied Charles Darwin in 1836 with
the germ of the idea for the theory of evolution. For
Malthus's very next paragraph gave a classic basis to
ecological thinking :

> "Through the animal and vegetable kingdoms, nature
> has scattered the seeds of life abroad with the most
> profuse and liberal hand. . . . Necessity, that imperious
> all-pervading law of nature, restrains them within the
> prescribed bounds. The race of plants and the race of
> animals shrink under this great restrictive law. And
> the race of man cannot, by any efforts of reason, escape
> from it. Among plants and animals its effects are
> waste of seed, sickness, and premature death. Among
> mankind, misery and vice . . ."

No one, after Malthus had written, could ever view the
human population problem out of relation to the problems
of food and other supplies provided with the assistance
of "nature". The ecological point had been made.[1]

Food is necessary to man ; there is no reason to dispute

[1] But see the reference in footnote 3, p. 90.

this postulate. But several observations on it are relevant.

First, food is not the only necessity of mankind; water, clothes, shelter and warmth are in different degrees prime necessities. Clearly, if the standard of life is to rise, the output of necessities must rise faster than the increase in population. Historical experience now affords, and had already afforded in Malthus's time, many examples of the production of food and other necessities increasing faster than population, and that without any distinct symptoms of increasing "misery and vice", but rather of their diminution.

It is important not to overlook necessities other than food. As a contemporary critic remarked, the absurdity of Malthus's doctrine might have been seen if he had stated it in respect of clothes.

The amount of food necessary to man varies, as is now known, within fairly narrow limits; even so, the limits widen according to the activities of the persons concerned, the climatic conditions and other factors. The *kind* of food required is of great importance. Improvements in dietary technique may be viewed rather like improvements in the arts of raising crops; better food is put into human beings, and they become more efficient animals. Thus the food (and other necessities) made available may affect the second postulate, interpreted as meaning the proclivity to have children in an imprudent manner, and also the conditions of the assumption that food production cannot be rapidly expanded. The postulates and the assumption are thus not independent of each other, as it is essential for Malthus's argument that they should be.

The second postulate, in the sense originally meant, was abandoned by Malthus himself when he admitted the possibility of "moral restraint". Those who refuse to class the extension of birth control, among married people especially, as vice, admit a further large class of exceptions to the generalization.

Once Malthus had admitted the check of "moral restraint" (which in his view consisted of virtuous abstention from marriage) the use of "the principle of population" as an argument against the ultimate perfectibility of mankind was no longer valid. Entirely different arguments had to be adduced, based on allegations as to the inability of working-class groups to exercise such restraint.

Malthus's argument against systems of equality thus changed its basis between the first and the later editions of his essay. Once he had admitted the possibility of checks to population growth which were neither miserable nor vicious his case against the "reform" of existing institutions, and his defence of the institution of private property, rested on the argument that prudential checks on population were in fact only possible in the context of the right kind of institutions. He argued that equality and common ownership of property were not conducive to moral restraint.[1] In this he may or may not have been right; the interesting point is that his case was now explicitly a *political* case (an instance of i in the notation of Table I above) and no longer rested on inexorable demological tendencies.

Despite these admissions, Malthus clung to his assumption of a geometrical population increase, which he claimed, in both the first and all later versions of the theory, to be consistent with observed fact. It was based, indeed, on the report that the population of certain colonies in North America had doubled in twenty-five years. Long after he had conceded the theoretical possibility of

[1] See Robbins, 1952, pp. 124–5.

moral restraint, Malthus clung to the belief that doubling in twenty-five years was the *natural* rate of increase of a population from which the special preventive checks associated with a shortage of food were removed. The article on "Population" in the *Encyclopædia* of 1824 returns to this same argument in more detail. "In an endeavour to determine the natural power of mankind to increase", the article states, ". . . we can have no other guide than past experience." We should expect, the article argues, the greatest natural increase where "room and nourishment were the most abundant". North America is a case in point; statistics for 1790, 1800 and 1810 confirm the view that natural doubling takes place in less than twenty-five years. This, then, is the "natural" rate of increase which any population will have.

Be it noted that Malthus in quoting these facts is not "reasoning from facts"; he is assuming that the one instance of an observed geometrical ratio is the "natural" ratio for all populations. He is assuming that this ratio would at once be attained by any other population with the like conditions of "room and nourishment". He is generalizing from a single instance. Thus a single instance of a population which had sufficient "room and nourishment" to multiply naturally at this rate, and did not in fact do so, would suffice to refute the assumption; and so would sufficient evidence of social forces capable of restricting the rate of natural increase of populations below his assumed rate, even though no instances had yet occurred. Little is still known of the precise social and economic forces affecting natural increase, but there is a wide enough experience of falling birth-rates among economically advanced populations to make it certain that his assumed geometrical ratio is wholly untrustworthy as a generalization of universal applicability.

The assumption of the ratios had to be abandoned by Malthus when he admitted that subsistence had in fact increased at times in a geometric ratio. As Cannan wrote: [1] "Deprived of the theory that the periodical additions to the average annual produce cannot possibly be increased, or, as Malthus preferred to put it, that subsistence can increase only in an arithmetical ratio, the *Essay on the Principle of Population* falls to the ground as an argument, and remains only a chaos of facts collected to illustrate the effects of laws which do not exist."

Cannan was perhaps too optimistic in thinking that the essay "falls to the ground", since Malthus had provided himself with the escape clause of allowing for "new starts in agriculture" (to explain "temporary" rises in standards of living).

But so long as "new starts" (i.e., improvements) continue to provide a higher standard of living, and to increase food and other necessities faster than the natural increase in population, there is no reason to regard growing population as the cause of inescapably increasing misery and vice for a large portion of mankind.

Perhaps an inkling of the reasons for Malthus's success as a controversialist may already have been gained. Although he abandoned the universality of his second postulate, and that of his assumption on the second ratio, he reiterated the universal applicability of his theory that there was a "tendency" for population and food supplies to grow at different rates, incompatible with each other.

§ 3. *Peculiarities of the Malthusian Doctrine.* Malthus's theory has thus two main aspects; it was conceived by a brilliant publicist who wished to attack existing social legislation, and also to attack "speculations" upon the

[1] *Op. cit.*, p. 144.

possible improvement of existing institutions of government and property; and, on the other hand, by a "philosopher" who first saw the importance of the limiting factors of environment on human material progress.

Malthus attached the highest importance to the geometrical and arithmetical ratios.

Marshall interpreted Malthus much too favourably when he stated that the arithmetical ratio was "really only a short way of stating the utmost that he thought any reasonable person could ask him to concede. What he meant, stated in modern language, was that the tendency to diminishing return, which is assumed throughout his argument, would begin to operate sharply after the produce of the island had been doubled. Doubled labour might give doubled produce; but quadrupled labour would hardly treble it . . . etc." [1]

The law of diminishing returns was not so modern that Malthus was unaware of it; on the contrary, Malthus himself enunciated the doctrine in his *Observation on the effects of the Corn Laws* in 1814 [2] a few months before West invented its "modern" name. He had a good reason for clinging to his "ratios" even in the later editions of his work on population. Diminishing returns might have been discussed in terms of facts—returns are sometimes diminishing, sometimes not. The ratios, on the other hand, can be asserted to be "tendencies" whether or not they are observable in a specific period.

Moreover, the concepts of diminishing returns in agriculture, and of the arithmetical ratio, are not quite the same thing. The arithmetical ratio applies to the total produce raised. What has to be asserted is that this total cannot be indefinitely doubled. The law of diminishing returns

---

1 Marshall, 1938, p. 179, footnote.
2 The date is given as 1815 in Sraffa's Introduction to Ricardo.

refers to the produce raised per head of labour, as more
and more poor land is brought into cultivation to meet
the needs of a growing population.   Diminishing returns
may operate without a failure to double the total produce.[1]
This is quite possible, and the income per head of a growing population may in such a case still rise if there are
increasing returns in manufacturing, so releasing enough
labour to offset diminishing returns in agriculture.
Malthus's ratio, crude as it was, looked beyond any such
"temporary" improvement; indeed, without reliance on
the ratios he could not have been sure of his inevitable
"misery".

Malthus's doctrine was not produced inductively but
deductively.   Thus, for example, as Malthus wrote: [2]
"One ingenious writer has remarked that I have not
deduced a single original fact from real observation to
prove the inefficiency of the checks which already prevail.
These remarks are correctly true, and are truisms exactly
of the same kind as the assertion that man cannot live
without food.   For undoubtedly as long as this continues
to be a law of his nature, what are here called the natural
checks cannot possibly fail of being effectual."

Yet Malthus's later claim to be reasoning from the facts
deceived so acute a critic as Alfred Marshall, whose piety
towards his forerunners on this point outweighed his
judgment.   He wrote of Malthus: [3]

"By a careful study of facts he proves that every
people, of whose history we have a trustworthy record,
has been so prolific that the growth of its numbers
would have been rapid and continuous if it had not

[1] Indeed, as re-stated by Ricardo, the L.D.R. operated mainly when
"wealth and population" were both increasing.
[2] See Cannan, 1924, p. 137.
[3] Marshall, 1938, p. 178.

8

been checked either by a scarcity of the necessaries of
life, or some other cause, that is, by disease, by war,
by infanticide, or lastly by voluntary restraint."

The transitions in Malthus's argument from a deductive
theory to an inductive one included a series of qualifications to the original theory. These were very fully
developed in the later editions of the essay. The resulting
modified theory was, however, incapable of either disproof
or verification.

Malthus, in his first essay, had *assumed* that population
always "tended" to increase faster than food "unless
there were checks", and he had *assumed* further that food
determined (with certain qualifications elaborated later)
the rate of growth actually observed. These assumptions
are in principle unverifiable. It is not necessary for
population ever to increase faster than food for his theory
to be true; indeed, as he sometimes remarked, according
to the second of these assumptions in his own theory, it
could not do so. The "tendency" of the population to
increase faster than food could therefore never be observed. The only tendency that could be observed was
that population always increased at exactly the same rate
as food. But, according to Malthus, observations on this
point were not really necessary since the truth of it was
self-evident.

What, then, of the numerous examples that could be
brought of rises taking place in the standard of life? At
this point Malthus introduced one of his famous after-
thoughts. It appeared that, after all, social custom and
the institutions of society had some effect on the amount
of food that the average working-man consumed. As an
example of a rise in the standard of living *not* offset by an
increase in population, the history of rural England in

the early years of the eighteenth century might well be quoted.

What is rather astonishing is that Malthus quoted the example himself:

> "It is well known," he wrote,[1] "that during this period the price of corn fell considerably, while the wages of labour are said to have risen. . . . From 1720 to 1750 the price of wheat had so fallen, while wages had risen, that instead of two-thirds the labourer could purchase the whole of a peck of wheat with a day's labour. . . . This great increase of command over the necessaries of life did not, however, produce a proportionate increase of population."

How did this fit into the Malthusian theory?   Because, of course, there *must have been* "prudential habits" among the workers, attributable to "civil liberty", which in turn depends upon "political liberty".[2]

Thus Malthus did not assert that the output of food could never increase faster than the growth of population. He merely asserted, and assumed, that when it did so the explanation must be "prudence" (i.e., the preventive check) or the fortuitous onset of some of the positive checks (wars or epidemics).   He defined a situation where (*a*) the standard of life was rising, and (*b*) there were no positive checks as an instance of the preventive check at work, and having thus assumed his result he could never be proved wrong.

The Report of the Royal Commission on Population states [3] that Malthus's argument rested on "two assumptions" not in fact realized, namely, (1) that technical

---

[1] Malthus, 1820, chap. iv, Sec. II, pp. 253–4.
[2] *Ibid.*, p. 251.
[3] Cmd. 7695, par. 264.

improvement in agriculture could only proceed very slowly, and (2) that imports would only make a minor contribution to a country's food supply.

Malthus would not for one moment have conceded that his argument rested on either one of these assumptions, both of which he considered quite fully at various points in his work.

It might, of course, be argued that Malthus's conclusion could only be justified if assumption (1) was true, in other words that Malthusianism only made sense if, historically, the law of diminishing returns was operating continuously. But this would be to change Malthus's doctrine completely and make it a historical statement on the law of diminishing returns. The *Encyclopædia Britannica* [1] article on "Population" states his position well:

"It has already been stated, that while land of good quality is in great abundance, the rate at which food might be made to increase would far exceed what is necessary to keep pace with the most rapid increase of population which the laws of nature in relation to human kind permit. But if society were so constituted as to give the fullest scope possible to the progress of cultivation and population, all such land, and all lands of moderate quality, would soon be occupied; and when the future increase of the supply of food came to depend upon the taking of very poor land into cultivation, and the gradual and laborious improvement of the land already cultivated, the rate of increase of food would certainly have a greater resemblance to a decreasing geometrical ratio than an increasing one. The yearly increment of food would, at any rate, have a constant tendency to diminish . . ."

[1] Malthus, 1824, p. 313.

The useful word "tendency" is later reiterated in italics:

> "While improvements in agriculture, accompanied by a great demand for labour and produce, might for some time occasion a rapid increase of food and population at a later period, in the same manner as if cultivation had been in an earlier stage of their progress."

(Malthus would have been in no way abashed by a period which he did not "foresee", since he was convinced on *a priori* grounds that "after a period" the pressure of population on food would show itself again.)

> "These variations," the article continued, ". . . obviously arise from causes which do not impeach the general *tendency* of a continued increase of produce in a limited territory to diminish the *power* of increase in future."

Thus Malthus conceded [1] that there was a possibility of "fresh starts" in agriculture, that is of technical progress. But he held that if this possibility was realized the day of reckoning was merely postponed, and perhaps aggravated in its effects, since each "fresh start" would, other things being equal, give rise to an even greater population. (This was a position in flat contradiction to his view that the crisis had already begun.)

Before leaving this point, it must be granted to the authors of the Royal Commission Report that undoubtedly they are giving a fair picture of what was *probably* Malthus's view of the immediate future. To quote again from the *Encyclopædia* article:

> "If, setting out from a tolerably well peopled country

[1] Moreover, he made the same point at greater length in both early and later editions of the Essay.

such as England, France, Italy, or Germany, we were
to suppose that, by great attention to agriculture, its
produce could be permanently increased every twenty-
five years by a quantity equal to that which it at
present produces, it would be allowing a rate of increase
decidedly beyond any probability of realization. The
most sanguine cultivators could hardly expect that, in
the course of the next two hundred years, each farm
in this country would produce eight times as much food
as it produces at present. . . . Yet this would be an
arithmetical progression, and would fall short, beyond
all comparison, of the natural increase of population in
a geometrical progression, according to which the
inhabitants of any country in 500 years, instead of
increasing to twenty times, would increase to above a
million times their present numbers."

This passage, and others similar to it, suggest that *probably* Malthus took a gloomy view of the future agricultural
capacity of the world. But he, at least, and later many
neo-Malthusians, were careful not to tie down the argument to any particular figure or to any particular forecast as to the actual rate of agricultural progress. It cannot be too often reiterated that his argument was *a priori*,
and general, depending upon a dogmatic statement that
a geometrical ratio would apply to humanity's natural
increase, while an arithmetical ratio applied to the increase in the food supply. That he *probably* foresaw an
early calamity can hardly be questioned—he would not
otherwise have had the brashness to forecast a disaster
to Godwin's system "within thirty years", and there are
many passages which suggest that he thought that
humanity in Western Europe and England could double
its numbers in twenty-five years successfully, but might

fail to double again in the next twenty-five; but he did not base his theory on any specific forecast, but used these figures illustratively. Had his theory been concerned with two periods of doubling only, as logically it should have been,[1] the argument would have been much clearer, and could have been afterwards tested by facts.

Malthus is sometimes supposed to have "taken for granted" that "imports would only make a minor contribution to a country's food supply". It seems odd that Malthus, who was in close private discussion, correspondence and public controversy with David Ricardo, and other leading economists, for at least ten years, on the subject of the importation of "corn" into Britain, should have been supposed to have given no consideration to this possibility. Malthus, of course, fully entertained the prospect of a heavy increase in food imports. He argued, however, that any alleviation to his "principle" gained in this way would be "temporary", meaning by this yet again that, at best, such a remedy would only postpone the evil day. In an early edition of his work there occurs the passage about "corn from America",[2]

---

[1] Because the famous geometrical ratio could not in fact operate beyond the third term (Malthus himself admitted this) according to the first postulate of his own argument.

[2] "In the wildness of speculation it has been suggested (of course, more in jest than in earnest) that Europe ought to grow its corn in America, and devote itself solely to manufactures and commerce . . . But even on the extravagant supposition that the natural course of things might lead to such a division of labour for a time, and that by such means Europe could raise a population greater than its lands could possibly support, the consequences ought justly to be dreaded. When upon this principle America began to withdraw its corn from Europe, and the agricultural exertions of Europe were inadequate to make up the deficiency, it would certainly be felt that the temporary advantages of a greater degree of wealth and population (supposing them to have been really attained) had been very dearly purchased by a long period of retrograde movements and misery."

while the maturer statement of his views in the *Encyclopædia* states:

> "It will be said, perhaps, that many parts of the earth are as yet very thinly peopled. . . . This is unquestionably true. Some parts of the earth would no doubt be capable of producing food at such a rate as to keep pace *for a few periods* [i.e. for some 'periods' (length unspecified) of doubling] with an unrestricted increase of population."

Those who think that Malthus ventured on a prophecy that has since been falsified are underrating his skill as a controversialist. This would be a point of mere historicism were it not for the consequence that neo-Malthusians may correctly claim that their forerunner has not been refuted by the facts. The facts cannot refute Malthus, since his theory was either:

(a) a statement based upon assumed postulates. In this case the only relevant argument is as to the universal applicability of those postulates. Once they are shown not to be universally true the theory loses all force as an inexorable law; or

(b) a modified and qualified historical generalization that is in principle unverifiable.

§ 4. *The "Qualified" Malthusian Doctrine.* There were three important qualifications,[1] finally, which distinguish the Malthusian doctrine from a strict historical prophecy or forecast. They are very difficult to pin down because they were stated many times with different variations.

First, there is the very loose definition of the "checks"

---

[1] Just how early these qualifications were developed by Malthus is a point of textual criticism that may be left aside; undoubtedly, in the course of controversy greater emphasis was placed on them.

on population, both preventive and positive.   Once the existence of "checks" of varying force is admitted the doctrine ceases to be a statement about what *will* happen, and merely a statement about "tendencies".   The existence of loosely defined checks then allows the Malthusian to fit any set of facts into the theory.   A "tendency" for all populations to increase "geometrically" is alleged, and any instances to the contrary can be dismissed, without further enquiry, as cases of the operation of a positive check, or perhaps of a preventive check. After all, the degree of misery and vice in a community cannot readily be measured; if the main reason for the failure of the population to increase at the geometrical rate seems to be a low birth-rate the preventive check can be assumed, and if the reason is a high death-rate a positive check is invoked.   Ah, says the Malthusian, that merely proves that the theory fits all the facts.   Unfortunately, it fits too many facts; it fits, indeed, all *conceivable* facts.   The "tendency" of the population to increase at a fixed geometrical ratio is alleged whatever the rates at which actual populations are growing in any circumstances.   If, for example, there is abundant food available and yet the natural increase falls short of Malthus's assumed maximum rate, and the death rate is low, then *by definition* the preventive check must be operating, and so on for any other example that may be chosen.

Moreover, the positive checks are just as elastic (and circular in reasoning) as the preventive.   Examples of what may be called "misery and vice" can no doubt be found in all human populations.   So long as "premature death" exists in any form whatsoever (and in a sense all deaths are premature), the Malthusian apologist can claim to discover positive checks that operate to prevent population increase from reaching its "natural" maximum.

Godwin had very much the worst of his arguments with Malthus because of this defensive strength in the Malthusian position. In his first counter-attack, indeed, he even conceded the "principle of population". When he returned to the attack in 1820, though aided by the statistician Booth, he adopted the wrong approach. He asked,[1] "if Mr. Malthus's doctrine is true, why is the globe not peopled?" and devoted chapters to the different major portions of the globe to investigate this issue at length. But the existence, *by definition*, of either preventive or positive checks provided an answer to this line of attack.

Much more effective and subtle were Nassau Senior's letters to Malthus.[2] He raised the much more awkward dilemma of how, if Malthus's theory were generally valid, the standard of life in many countries had gone up over the centuries. He wrote:

"... the only difference between us is one of nomenclature. You would still say, that in the absence of disturbing causes, population has a *tendency* to increase faster than food, because the comparative increase of the former is a mere compliance with our natural wishes, the comparative increase of the latter is all effort and self-denial. I should still say, that, in the absence of disturbing causes, food has a tendency to increase faster than population, because, in fact, it has generally done so, and because I consider the desire of bettering our condition as natural a wish as the desire of marriage."

Malthus replied that:

"Whether population were actually increasing faster than food, or food faster than population, it was true

[1] *Op. cit.*, 1820, p. 20.
[2] Quoted by Smith, 1951, p. 184.

that, except in new colonies, favourably circumstanced, population was always pressing against food, and was always ready to start off at a faster rate than that at which the food was actually increasing."

Any improvement in food supply, he thought, would "soon" be swallowed up in increased numbers.

This brings the argument to the second of Malthus's major qualifications of his doctrine, the period within which it was supposed to become demonstrable to all.

In the first essay, and indeed in all later versions of the theory, Malthus insisted that the evils consequent upon the "principle of population" were already pressing and urgent.   Thus the *Encyclopædia* article of 1824 states: [1]

"The pressure arising from the difficulty of procuring subsistence is not to be considered a remote one, which will be felt only when the earth refuses to produce any more, but as one which not only exists at present over the greatest part of the globe, but, with few exceptions, has been almost constantly acting upon all the countries of which we have any account."

This would seem to tie the theory down to a historical generalization that could be tested.   The actual broad facts of history were the reverse, as Nassau Senior pointed out.

Simultaneously with the view that population pressure was always observably pressing on food, were the arguments about "tendencies", about a prisoner being restrained by the walls of a prison even though the walls were not touching him, and about "periods" of doubling —it being a matter of no moment whether one or two

[1] *Op. cit.*, p. 316.

had to be conceded before the crisis arrived. Indeed the very same *Encyclopædia* article on population spoke of the principle in terms of farms not being able to produce on an average more than eight times their present output over the next two hundred years.

Thus Malthus introduced the qualification that his principle might not work out for some hundreds of years, and stated the ratios in such broad terms that they could not be justified except over hundreds of years; yet at the same time he remained dogmatically convinced that the time of reckoning had already come and that the "checks" had always operated.

This double position is not formally a self-contradiction; it *might* be true that the ratios worked out infallibly only over centuries, and also that there was already population pressure everywhere. But the two are really quite separate arguments, and Malthus's qualifications succeeded in inextricably muddling them together. *If* the problem is one of centuries, then the real questions are: just what are the forces making for population doubling (increasing at a given rate) and for food and other necessaries doubling (increasing at a given rate)? This question can hardly be settled by a dogmatic assertion that the one always "tends to" double faster than the other (in the absence of increasing vice and misery).

If, on the other hand, the problem is a current one, that population increase has outrun the supply of food and necessaries, then the correct question is: what has caused this ill-balance? Can any humane steps be taken to remedy the situation? Do laws need to be passed, or institutions improved? No, says the earlier Malthus, because any improvement is short-lived; and in any case laws and institutions are but froth on the deep irresistible stream of the life forces making for population pressure.

But now comes Malthus's third qualification.[1]

Surprisingly, in view of the original purpose of his work, he emphasized the dependence of the actual level of population upon the laws, institutions and habits of each society. Indeed, he went so far as to invoke these factors to account for the present "*scanty* population of the earth",[2] remarking that there were few large countries where the population might not be double, triple, ten or a hundred times what it actually was "if the institutions of society, and the moral habits of the people" had been favourable to such an increase (meaning to a sufficient increase in food cultivation).

This concession gave away everything that had originally been at issue. Hazlitt's question, reiterated in a different form by Nassau Senior, now became unanswerable; how could the "principle" be an answer to Godwin and others? Are we to believe, in Hazlitt's words, that "if reason should ever get the mastery of all our actions, we shall then be governed entirely by our physical appetites and passions, without the least regard to the consequences"? Has reason no power over the impulse to propagate?

If, as Malthus had to concede, the arithmetical rate of increase can be laid aside, why assume that the *numerical value* of the rate of population increase would be insensately, and not temperately, increased to meet the changed circumstances?

Malthus's argument really now boiled down to two generalizations (current and future population pressure) based on the one instance of the North American population. It was as though an investigation were carried out into the "natural appetite" of men. Ten

1 Malthus, 1820, chap. iv, sec. II.
2 *Encyclopædia*, 1824, p. 316.

men would be set down in front of large dinners; one of the men would have plenty of room for his food, having had a morning of heavy exercise—he might eat 1,200 calories. The other nine would eat varying less amounts (and might be provided with less amounts). Malthus concludes that "natural appetite" is 1,200 calories. All men would eat 1,200 calories if it were placed before them. If, then, in a second experiment the 1,200 calories are placed before the other nine and they do not eat it they are alleged, by definition, to be either sick (owing to misery or vice) or capable of unusual moral restraint. Natural appetite as a concept is not re-examined.

The power of increase of population is thus thought of as something that is given and unchangeable; in Malthus's system it is only *revealed* when food is plentiful, but it is not a *function* of plenty of food. Its force is the same whether there is plenty of food or not. Malthus's theory was not based on belief that a population's power to increase was a function of changing food supply, but that *actual* population increase was a function of this variable.

Since Malthus's time no *theory* of population has been invented. It has for many years been recognized, for instance, that modern war is not a check to population in the Malthusian sense at all.[1] Yet the teaching of Malthus is still often assumed to apply to modern society. But if war is not a check on population, is it wise to assume that "misery and vice" in all their forms are checks either? May not the power of increase of population be an increasing function of "misery and vice" (or, at least, of some specific forms of misery and vice)? In this case a more direct attack on these things, even by way of mere alleviation in the first instance, may be a good way of reducing any existing pressure of population upon food.

[1] See Wright, 1923, p. 136.

Steps, however small, towards a more "perfect" human society may be far from impracticable, and indeed the only sensible steps to take to meet the world's population problems.

The clear alternative to Malthus's theory is the hypothesis that economic as well as social conditions affect the growth and size of populations, and that sexual passions operate only within the restrictions or stimuli imposed by these conditions.

§ 5. Neo-Malthusianism.

Neo-Malthusians sometimes argue that there is perhaps a lessened moral obligation on Western nations to provide scientific aid to backward nations because it can probably be demonstrated that a sudden increase of population in those nations will lead to disaster.[1] Such an obligation, it may well be agreed, is not to be regarded as unconditional *if* it can be shown that the result of such aid would be an increase in population so sudden that famines of an incurable kind would result.

India is the example that is most frequently cited. But can anyone argue that India's increasing population has, mainly because of its increase, been a prime cause of international tension and disorder? This purely political argument could hardly be sustained from the record of international exchanges at the United Nations Assembly. There is no doubt that the rapid increase of India's population creates a problem for India, and for its neighbours and for other countries, but that this is one of the major causes of the international tension in the world since 1945 is not demonstrable. It might of course become so, but so might a number of other demographic changes, and all sorts of degrees of demographic

[1] Hill, 1952, p. 93.

pressure have been made the excuse for expansionist and aggressive policies. But the increase in itself does not necessarily demand a warlike solution. Indeed, the other neo-Malthusian argument which is most frequently encountered is precisely contrary to this; namely, that a sudden increase of population will undermine the physique of the people concerned, and impoverish them. This is a more realistic fear.

The Axis powers used population pressure as an excuse for aggression. But the objective of their rulers was power, not room for peaceful expansion. The Germans and Japanese wanted to acquire territories in which the birth-rate was higher than their own, and so did the Italian government to a lesser extent. The Japanese allowed Manchuria to fill up with Chinese faster than with Japanese, as being a more readily exploitable labour force; the Germans fell back on genocide, not to find room for unemployed Germans but to establish strategically placed loyal populations in conquered territory. The rulers of two of these countries encouraged a high birth-rate to further their ambitions.

When Western publicists express the fear that the increase of Eastern populations may make it hard for "civilization itself to survive" it is difficult not to entertain the suspicion that they are identifying "civilization" not with defined and recognizable qualities of life but with the predominance of certain social groups. Otherwise it is difficult to make any sense of the fears that they express as to the needs of the backward areas. How, they sometimes ask, can India be supported if its population rises in the next thirty years to 700 millions? [1] For if the

[1] This was the figure mentioned by Professor Hill in 1944 in an address to the India-Burma Association on "India: Scientific Development or Disaster." Quoted by Bertram, 1949.

Indian standard of life goes up, as it well may, and mortality rates fall, more food per head will then be needed, and India will consume some three times the amount then that it consumes to-day (in 1944 the population of India was put at some 430 millions).

Evidently it is no longer the welfare of the Indian that is at stake. His standard of living has gone up, *ex hypothesi*, and his mortality rate has gone down. The argument is political, and not economic or biological.

Yet another form of the same neo-Malthusian reasoning is the inappropriate comparison between Oriental and American methods of production and standards of living. This argument takes two forms: first, how can world resources possibly meet the enormous claim on raw materials that will arise if these numerous Eastern peoples raise their economic requirements per head to anything approximating the present consumption per head of the average U.S. citizen?

And, secondly, how can an Eastern farmer (say a Chinese) be induced to get any benefit, on his subsistence farm, from a tractor, or modern agricultural machinery, when he produces virtually no cash crops at all?

Both of these arguments usually come from physical scientists with little or no training in economics or the social sciences generally. It is very useful that they have raised these questions, since puzzling over the issues that have to be settled may not be unprofitable. But the notion that the questions in themselves provide *a priori* proof of over-population is not strictly tenable.

Why should the economic advance of any backward country, say India, follow the same path as has been followed by the United States? Reflection suggests that this is historically quite impossible. Because it is impossible there is no likelihood that India will absorb

9

raw materials per head at the same rate of increase as the United States has exhibited. That particular phenomenon can hardly be repeated in the Argentine or Brazil, let alone in the Far East. Is there, then, any excuse for deliberately withholding medical or scientific knowledge from India in order that its mortality rate should be maintained?

For reasons of social organization, which has varied from country to country, many economically "backward" countries have been organized on the basis of the family, and on the basis of the large family; there have been social checks placed on unlimited multiplication (marriage restrictions, sometimes infanticide, and sometimes practices of abstention) for centuries, but it so happens that social organization has been in many places framed to encourage population increase.[1]

Farming in parts of China reached very high levels of output per acre. It is true that the Chinese peasant farmer, in an almost cashless economy, could not afford a power disc, a battery of grain drills, a combine or a fifty horse-power machine,[2] or even to hire an aeroplane to sow his seeds from the air, but he could raise twice the product per acre of the American farmer with all these advantages. Some parts of China suffered from erosion, but the farmer on the loess soils could produce crop after crop (like his Western European opposite number) without exhausting the fertility of the land, even without the aid of manures.

This is not to say that the Chinese farmer was on balance efficiently organized. In the long history of China the social forces had strongly favoured an increase of population to a point that was very high indeed in

1 Pan, Chia-lin and Taeuber, 1952.
2 Smith, J. R., 1949, p. 359.

relation to the land politically and geographically available for peaceful cultivation.   But the balance of advantage as between him and his American equivalent was less obviously on the American side than the purely neo-Malthusian argument allows.   The American farmer needed a vast industrial organization to back him up, and this organization, too, had its bottlenecks.   In so far as the germ of truth (which becomes distorted in neo-Malthusianism) is that "bottlenecks are to be feared" then it is not certain whether, in the long run, the highly mechanized farmer or the subsistence farmer (if he is on good soil) will feel the worse pinch first.

Are there really any good reasons, Malthusian or otherwise, for agreeing that medical and scientific knowledge should be withheld from the backward populations? Various counter-arguments, in addition to the humane considerations so obvious as to be unnecessary to mention, can be brought against any such suggestion.

First,[1] it is much easier to make a vaccine for a million people than to re-equip them economically, or to educate them to operate new production and agricultural techniques.   This cuts both ways; it raises the danger, so much emphasized by the neo-Malthusians, that the health reform will be unsound, resting on "fragile foundations", since the necessary social changes that should have gone with it will not yet have taken place.   But, on the other hand, since this type of reform is easier to introduce than a more radical change, that in itself makes medical advance a good starting-point for a much wider programme of reform.

Moreover, the fight to reduce mortality will reduce

---

[1] In these two paragraphs I am much indebted to the summary arguments put forward by Professor Sauvy (*Théorie Générale*), 1952, p. 32.

morbidity as well in most circumstances. This ought to have the effect of increasing the productivity of labour. Secondly, to save a young man of eighteen years of age is to save an important capital investment (the economic waste of high death-rates among young people is often overlooked), and, thirdly, medical progress may indirectly reduce the level of fecundity.[1] Fourthly, until health conditions have been improved in backward communities little serious technical developments of other kinds can be expected, for the simple reason that the technicians will not be there (if they are in short supply they will seek employment elsewhere). Medical reform up to a certain standard is a prerequisite of economic progress.

The effect of a sudden reduction of mortality will raise different problems for different populations according to how they are already situated. It is true that where the standard of living is already low, and alternative means of employment difficult, a reduction in mortality by reason of a medical reform may cause an acute population problem, at least for some decades. But where the population is sparse, or where economic development of industry is possible, or where emigration is feasible, no such embarrassment need ensue; furthermore, in these circumstances a rapid decline in mortality may itself lead to social conditions in which fertility also rapidly declines.

Neo-Malthusianism goes much further than the reasonable claim that a sudden spurt in the size of a population *may* cause a decline in the standard of living. In its more extreme forms it claims that an ultimate decrease in the

[1] "The Indian born in 1931 had a life expectation of 26·5 years; the Englishman in the same year, a life expectation of 61 years. This meant that pre-war India spent 22·5 per cent of its national income on raising children who would make hardly any contribution to production, while England spent only 6·5 per cent of its national income on the raising of children." (See F.A.O., *The State of Food and Agriculture*, 1948, p. 31.)

standard of life for the world is inevitable, and this view is based on postulates analogous to Malthus's, if more severe and improbable.

The neo-Darwinian version of neo-Malthusianism starts from the proposition that man is a wild animal.[1] The machinery of the theory is the use of a limitless time-scale (a "million years", or, in other words, infinity—as long ahead as is needed for the result). But the conclusion from the theory is not timeless, or related to a remote future; it is related to present policy. For at any given moment, particularly the present, it is found convenient to divide the world into advanced ("good") populations, which multiply slowly and so secure and preserve a relatively high standard of life, and backward ("bad") populations that multiply fast, so threatening the existence of the good, civilized, small-family peoples. (Strictly speaking, the neo-Malthusians should count the Americans as a "bad" population since they have been historically among the fastest growing of peoples, but this is always ignored in their expositions.) The policy of the good civilized peoples must therefore be to check the increase of the backward peoples for the greater glory of civilization.

The modern neo-Malthusian has to explain how it is that standards of life have risen in large parts of the world despite an immense percentage increase in population, and why it is that populations in more primitive societies have not yet exhibited that wild animal rate of increase to which they are held, *a priori*, to be prone. On the first point they have to admit that what they call "local" or "unstable" advances in the standard of living have been gained, unstable because, *ex hypothesi*, any "good" population making such a gain will sooner or

[1] Darwin, 1952.

later be reduced again to penury by the multiplication in numbers of some inferior breed. The first population will then be crowded out of existence by the second, owing to the Gresham's law that bad populations drive out good.

Why cannot, even on these assumptions, some agreement, open or tacit, be made with the rising tide of lower type humans? Because, on the neo-Darwinian view, man is ultimately and always a wild animal that cannot be tamed, except in a very superficial and incomplete way. If such an agreement were made and kept, there would be always some more savage (more natural? at any rate a wilder) group which would take advantage of the truce to gain its ends by multiplication.

The whole case rests then, not on scientific experiment nor on observation, but on a doctrinaire view.

Once it is granted that man (or some man) has (and always will have) an incurable impulse to multiply regardless of consequences, the rest follows from the further supposition that ultimately food can only be available at an arithmetic increase, while (over a long enough period) man will multiply geometrically. But all that this shows is that man cannot double his numbers twice, unless food can double twice in the same intervals; as has already been seen. And if mankind once tried the experiment of multiplying faster than its maximum rate, with a consequent loss of income, it might, in most people's view, learn something from the experience. Even without the experience there seems no good reason to suppose that peoples multiply with the crass disregard of supplies that is assumed. Whole societies have learned to limit their numbers (as even the neo-Darwinians admit) and it cannot be proved that other societies are inherently unable to learn the same lesson.

The strength of the neo-Darwinian case lies in the resuscitation of the indefinite time-scale. However clearly the social scientist demonstrates that one population after another has been able to limit its rate of growth, the neo-Darwinian can always retort: "Well, maybe this time, or next time, or the time after; but what if world population reaches ten-fold its present size? Then, you must concede, things will be getting pretty awkward, and if not at ten-fold then at some multiple my case must be allowed, and I can go as high as I please."

This argument is spurious because it assumes what it is necessary to prove. Hypothetically, it may be conceded that there is some size of population which would be too great for the world's resources to maintain since these are believed to be finite. But what is not conceded is that the inevitable doubling process should be indefinitely followed. During even the next fifty years mankind's economic and educational institutions and his social structure may well be modified along lines that are now quite unpredictable. We cannot say anything very useful about these institutions as they will exist in one hundred years' time, although we may speculate upon them. When the time-scale is extended to a thousand, a hundred thousand, or a million years, prediction is still more unreliable. It is not only pointless, but unworthy of science, to pretend that man's behaviour in the matter of reproduction can be predicted for centuries ahead.

§ 6. *Equality of Population with Food.* Food is in general a relatively perishable commodity, and only in recent years have methods of long-period storage become practicable. It follows that food is one of the goods that have to be produced concurrently with consumption, except for such storage as is necessary to tide over from harvest to harvest. In this respect food differs from clothes, books, wine and houses, and from most forms of capital goods used in production.

The agricultural industry has, moreover, always tended to be highly competitive.

For both these reasons it is usually uneconomic, and sometimes disastrously so, for the producers, to produce more food in a year than can be currently consumed. It follows that, in reasonably well-organized economies, the food production is roughly equal to the available effective demand. So long as all members of the community have a sufficiency of purchasing-power, the amount of food produced will usually satisfy need, but, for the reasons given, will not greatly exceed it. Thus, historically, in all periods of reasonably "viable" economic organization, the food supply will be roughly sufficient to equal the needs of the population; it is an illusion to suppose that, for this reason of equality alone, the population must have adjusted itself to the volume of the food supply.

This illusion is one all neo-Malthusians are prone to mistake for reality; of course, an equality of population with food *might* be due to an adjustment in population, but the point is that such an equality is by no means a proof that such an adjustment has taken place.

For most civilized communities there is fairly strong contributory evidence to suggest that the adjustment is of food to population and not the other way round. In all but the most primitive communities there are considerable economic resources devoted to many other satisfactions lower down in the scale of necessities than food, even for the consumption of the poorer classes, and still more so for the better off and the very rich. These populations might sacrifice some of their relatively luxurious consumption rather than starve, or support a "starving margin". If they choose a set of institutions which allows a starving margin to exist side by side with resources that could be used to produce food but are not so used, it is a stretch of language to argue that the starving margin is the consequence of an unconquerable difficulty in producing food, and those who hold that, on the contrary, bad institutions are the cause of misery, vice, starvation and war would seem to have the better of this particular argument.

§ 7. *Neo-Godwinianism.* Many writers and thinkers of to-day ascribe starvation, famine, high death-rates among children, and disease not to population maladjustment but to the inefficiency and injustice of the social institutions operative in the regions concerned. This approach may, with some historical accuracy, be labelled neo-Godwinianism, because although there is a diversity of views on how to reform society there is a common Godwinian standpoint taken up in response to the neo-Malthusian challenge; all such writers agree that human institutions and not the inexorable laws of nature are at fault wherever grave social evils are found.

In its crudest form neo-Godwinianism can degenerate into a theory as circular and non-operational as the modified Malthusian theory. Godwinianism of this kind can be neither supported nor refuted by any conceivable set of facts. If it is alleged that all human ills are the consequence *by definition* of some human institution that is unjust (or of some flaw in the working of a just institution), then there is no more to be said. The definition of an unjust human institution has been given, and no instance of it can be proved to exist, or not to exist, as a consequence of finding with it the characteristic by which it is identified.

Some writers who attack in particular a social institution which they name "Colonialism" come dangerously near to this kind of circular reasoning. Malnutrition in an existing colony they can readily ascribe to colonialism; but what of Brazil or Calabria in Italy? To explain malnutrition there they must refer back to the results of colonialism that ceased long ago, or of a colonialism that is deemed to exist surreptitiously because of the social structure of the South of Italy. The cases of evident short-term over-population in Italy and Japan are, indeed, especially difficult for the anti-colonial theorists to explain, and they must have recourse to a definition of "Colonialism" so wide as to deprive the term of any precise meaning.

The neo-Godwinian view has the merit of recognizing that human institutions should be treated as a variable in the problem of population. It can hardly be denied that what is an "optimum population" for one set of institutional circumstances may be greater or less than what would be the optimum for a different set of circumstances, even though the raw materials available and the technical means of production remained the same.

But this only means that the problem of population is much more complex than it is made out to be by those who neglect the fact that social institutions are mutable. It does not mean that there is no population problem; it means that the problem may take many forms.

At some date in the future, possibly fifty, a hundred or a thousand years hence, the rate of population increase will have to slow down. Common sense indicates that it is possible that it will slow down without tyranny, misery or vice, in such a long period, since in many countries, with fairly tolerable social conditions, it has already slowed down.

Common sense indicates also that tyranny, misery and vice will be hard to eradicate.   However, this gives rise to a very different degree of fear from that which is due to the belief that, however hard people try, these social evils must always be with humanity, in a steadily intensified degree.

CHAPTER V

THEORIES OF STATIC EQUILIBRIUM

§ 1. *The Idea of a Maximum Population.* There can be only one optimum size of population, if the terminology of economics is correctly derived, although opinions will differ as to the criteria for it. But first the even more fundamental concepts of "maximum" and "minimum" populations need to be explained, and their usefulness discussed.

A maximum population occurs, in an isolated community, when the death-rate rises to the same level as the birth-rate, or more exactly, when the two rates come into equality with each other. Most people, whether Malthusians or not, believe that there is some definite upper limit to the size of population that a given "country", with given techniques of production, can support. What is implied is that at some point natural increase falls to zero.

Let us suppose that actual population, at any given time, is ON_1; then the common assumption that populations have a maximum can be expressed by saying that there is some larger size of population, say ON, beyond which further population increase is impossible. What is implied, then, is that as population expands to ON natural increase falls to zero, so that over some of the population range from ON_1 to ON natural increase must be a decreasing function of the size of population.

How would this come about? There are many possible causal links between size of population and birth- and death-rates. For biological or economic or political reasons death-rates may rise as population expands; or birth-rates may fall; or both movements may occur.   The only assumption that has to be made is that BR meets

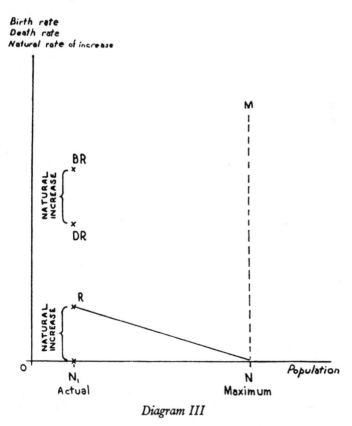

Diagram III

DR somewhere on the vertical line NM, which represents a population of the maximum size ON (Diagram III).

The analysis is timeless.   What is considered here is the functional relationship between vital rates and sizes of population. How long any particular adjustment would take to complete is a separate question.

The cases most commonly feared are those in which natural increase is reduced to zero wholly or partly because of a rise in mortality rates, this rise being due to a severe decline in the standards of living. With most age-distributions, this implies a rise in crude death-rates before maximum population is reached. A population that reached its maximum for this reason would be forced into a temporary (or if the situation persisted, a "permanent") stability of size, a stability clearly less favourable than one attained by population planning.

Equality of birth- and death-rates is a necessary but not a sufficient condition of a maximum population, for such an equality could be gained by a population which "chose" some point short of the maximum size, and maintained it by restricting its birth-rate to the ruling level of the death-rate.

Where equality of rates is enforced by circumstances— that is, where a maximum has been reached—savage restrictions on life must have been imposed. A condition prevails that there will literally be one extra death for every extra birth that occurs. This probably would mean either a very high infantile mortality rate, or infanticide, or an appalling disease rate among the old and helpless.

Thus the degree of misery implied by the "true maximum" is worse than that suffered in either India, Egypt or China, where all the populations still seem, after all, to be on the increase. The populations of these and other countries may be far nearer to the true maximum level than any humane person would want them to be, and far closer than is either desirable or necessary, but even so, these populations are not, as a whole, suffering the frightful conditions which a maximum would imply.

Emigration is the classic remedy when desperate or bold solutions are needed, and is perhaps in some cases analogous to the swarming of certain animal species. The "realized maximum" will be less than the "true maximum" if emigration takes place, and is reached when net emigration rates plus death-rates come into equality with the birth-rates (Diagram IV).

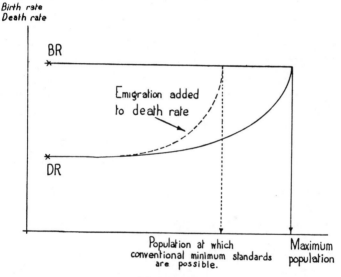

Diagram IV

Italy seems to have reached some kind of "realized maximum" about 1910, and Ireland in the 1840's and 1850's. Where any maximum actually occurs depends partly upon the conventional standards of living that people regard as tolerable before they emigrate. Evidently, although in the nineteenth century England and Wales, Germany and other European countries were sources of net emigration their populations still grew, and were far smaller than either the "realized" or the horrific "true" maximum.

The economic problem of the real world is not, then, in practice that of meeting the imminent danger of a maximum being reached, but that of meeting the needs of a greatly increasing population wherever it happens to be expanding. For such a population seeks not only food but employment, not only clothes but sound government, not only water supplies but amusement and transport; it has to be housed, if only in hovels or caravans, at least on land, either within the state's existing boundaries in new urban expansions or conurbations or in more densely peopled agricultural districts, or abroad amid some alien culture.

No wonder that the torrent of natural increase has led to some signs of panic among those upon whom leadership or responsibility has fallen! But the problem has to be looked at as one of reorganization to meet a current increase in numbers, not as one that is intrinsically insoluble, despite the complexities that it raises, which will no doubt strain human ingenuity very seriously.

§ 2. *The Idea of a Minimum Population.* The problems of the isolated community offer several parables of much wider application than to the special issue of rural depopulation. In the first place, any consideration of them must throw into relief the importance of external economies, that is, of the complementarity of different services provided not only within the same industry but by different industries. The village grows large enough to support a doctor, a baker and a cobbler, and their advent in turn makes possible the arrival of a newsagent, and so on; and as the community grows, so an improved transport service, drainage system, water supply, post office, milk delivery and other simple advantages accrue.

For example, if an island off the west coast of Scotland depends for its health on the services of a doctor, it follows that the island cannot long remain inhabited should those services be withdrawn. If the island is so remote, and transport to it so difficult, that the doctor cannot look to other patients for his emoluments, the island must have a certain minimum size of population for his services to be retained. Should it fall in numbers below that minimum size, those services are withdrawn, and the population will leave or fail to survive (if left in complete isolation) on the presumption that live births must fall and the death-rate increase.

There are not only economic limitations of this kind to the economic viability of an isolated population, but also biological limitations. The age-distribution (and birth-rates) must be such that a sufficiency of the population is passing through the child-bearing ages (and having children) to replace those who die. These biological limits are of great interest in studying the survival possibilities of small, relatively homogeneous, racial groups, but in an economic study they need not be analysed in any detail.

Once the minimum has been exceeded a whole new host of possibilities open up. Thus economic advantages may be gained not necessarily continuously, but, as it were, in quanta, or by crossing "humps", discontinuous leaps forward. The community can support a policeman, and law and order improve; a school or theatricals, and education progresses. There are more and more humps to cross. Finally, if the village becomes a town or a city, the cross-relationships which permit increased efficiency in satisfying need may be yet more numerous, and indeed very difficult to trace and to identify.

The minimum, like the maximum, population is not absolute but depends upon the degree of organization assumed, and the standard of living that is accepted. Some groups might dispense with a baker; others would not.

Another example is that of the producer skilled in marketing, whose faculties would not be fully exploited until, for one reason or another, demand reached a certain size.[1] Above a certain size of market, the marketer's rôle would be different in kind, and not merely in degree. This argument has sometimes been used in connection with an increase in capital and hence of demand, which might lead to entirely new ways of combining factors of production; in other words, to a discontinuous leap forward on a path of economic progress. The same reasoning can be applied to population growth. Population growth may either take place at the same rate as, or less fast than, the growth of capital, i.e., if the whole economic system has expanded. Either provides the possibility of increasing returns, which may indeed accrue even when population changes faster than capital.

The degree to which increasing returns may be realized is not a mere technical question, but a question of economics, theoretical and applied, that is of a generalized theory of economic growth and of a review of the specific investments to be made. In that light the size of the optimum must be discussed.

§ 3. *The Optimum Population on Static Assumptions.* The term "optimum population" was frequently used in the economic literature between World War I and the Great

---

[1] Robbins, 1934, p. 13.

Depression.[1]   Most writers defined the optimum population more or less explicitly as the size of population consistent with maximum economic welfare.[2]   It was recognized by some that the term "maximum economic welfare" involved questions of the distribution as well as of the production of real income, and that this difficulty already gave some ambiguity to the concept.   The size of the optimum was thought, in general, to be determined by the availability of natural resources per head for varying actual sizes of population, and by the facilities that existed for economic co-operation, both internally to an area and in relation to the inhabitants of other areas.

The detailed history of the idea of the (static) optimum cannot be given here.[3]   Cannan first formulated it in this way:[4]

"... At any given time the population which can exist on a given extent of land, consistently with the attainment of the greatest productiveness of industry possible at that time, is definite."

He gave the theory more precision (and a name) in his later work.   Carr-Saunders used the idea in his discussions of actual populations.

The notion was often stated in terms of production per head, not of welfare.   For example,[5] it would be argued that an area was over-populated when returns per head were less in that area than they would have been if the populations had been a little smaller.   This point had, of course, nothing to do with the point at which any visible

[1] Keynes began the debate with some remarks in the second chapter in his *Economic Consequences of the Peace*, 1920.
[2] See, for example, Chapter 3 of Cannan, 1928, and Dalton, 1928, p. 28.
[3] A large part of it was summarized excellently by Professor Robbins in his essay on the theory, 1927.
[4] Cannan, 1888, p. 22.
[5] See Robbins, 1927, p. 120.

pressure on the means of actual subsistence had appeared; the optimum was passed once real output per head began to fall.

Reflection on how precisely to define the optimum led to the refinement of the concept, but at the same time to its being criticized as of little value. It was thought to be highly artificial to select "average real income" as the one test of an "optimum"—so many other facets of life were omitted from the concept; it was thought misleading because population movements were dynamic, and because changing numbers were alleged to be more important than size; it was criticized because it abstracted from age-distribution problems (on a first statement); it was derided because, as usually stated, it had abstracted from direct consideration of problems arising from international trade, and from changes in industrial technique. These criticisms effectively debarred the static concept of the optimum from a fashionable rebirth in the discussions that preceded the Population Report of 1949.

All these objections are, however, really one objection: that which is made to the static abstract analysis of population problems. That such an analysis has its limitations is important to remember, but that this should be an absolute deterrent to a cautious use of the technique may be disputed.

Possible objectives for a single political unit might be the maximization of:

(*a*) power;
(*b*) income per head for a section, or class, of the community;
(*c*) expectation of life (over-all average, or the average for a class);
(*d*) economic security;
(*e*) output per head.

If each of these objectives is considered in turn it will be found that even this five-fold classification is insufficient. Within each of the five divisions there are further alternatives—different ends to choose from—and there are yet other headings altogether outside the five here listed.

The optimum size of population will be larger very often in a society of exploiters and exploited than in one of equal abilities and equal rights, for reasons that can be worked out quite adequately by the device of a total product curve. The total product curve, which is in effect a quantum index relating national product to number of workers available (some fraction, not necessarily constant, of total population being deemed to comprise the working population), may shift over time, and have to be entirely redrawn.

The new product curve might present a different possible optimum by any of the criteria. Greatest possible output per head might now be attained with a greater or less working population than before. Thus a general rise in productivity can be shown not *necessarily* to lead to the disappearance of all population problems, since after such a rise it may happen that the optimum size of population is smaller than before (although *any* population may now have the capacity to be better off).

At any given moment, in relation to that somewhat abstract idea of "total product", an actual working, and total, population is probably rather too small or too large. It could hardly be expected that population size should remain exactly right for long, except by extraordinary luck, since underlying techniques are so constantly changing.

In war-time, populations usually seem to be too small, partly because of military demands, partly because of the needs of industrial production. In peace-time they seem sometimes to be too large, perhaps because of a sluggish economic demand for the services of labour, or the failure of individuals, or of the state, to provide some rather necessary amenities (e.g., schools, houses or water), or because of sudden fluctuations in external trading conditions.

What should be sought, however, is the optimum that is justified by long-term rather than short-term conditions of demand and supply.   But the static optimum for, say, 1980 may be inconsistent with natural increase changes from the static optimum at some other date; and, in discussing possible optima, dates, as well as economic institutions, have to be assumed as part of the essential framework of reference.

§ 4. *Ecological Equilibrium.*   The propagation and the nourishment of different organisms are both co-operative and competitive processes.   So soon as the relative extent of this co-operation and competition is known it is possible to predict the ecological equilibrium size of any particular population in relation to all the others.   The trick is to discover the functional relationships between the size of population A and the size of population B, C, D, etc.; once all these were known, and if it could be assumed that all populations tend to increase in the given environment of the earth, all populations could be predictable.   Some of these functional relationships are known and others are being discovered.   But man is busy modifying the functions themselves.   He is always aiming to disturb the "natural" ecological balance in favour of some favourite objective of his that he has in mind.   (He thinks that he is acting in his own interest, but is not always correct in this view.)   Any reasoning from ecology as to the future of human populations has to be qualified by remarking that (*a*) the environment laid down by the original functions is being changed, and (*b*) human populations may choose not to expand to the limit.

At a given date (or over a short period) the functional relationships may, however, be taken to be constant, and, as a first approximation, some static relationships can be worked out. At a later stage in the exercise we can speculate about the time needed, in principle, for the adjustments towards any equilibrium to be made. At the moment we are concerned only with the sizes of different populations that are consistent with each other, not with their rates of change.

A well-known example of this type of reasoning is the parable of a Juan Fernandez type of island, where grass is supposed to be available to support goats, and the goats support wolves. The goats live on the grass and thrive until the wolves arrive, the number of goats depending upon the amount of grass available. A pair of wolves, left on the island by some careless sea-captain, batten on the goats and drive them to the rocky hills in the centre of the island. If the wolves successfully pursue the goats and exterminate them, they doom themselves to early extinction. If the agility of the goats develops sufficiently for a minimum number of them to survive, then an ecological balance is struck between the maximum number of goats that the wolves can pick off from time to time, and the maximum number of wolves that can survive on this wearisome diet.

This story has sometimes been used to support the Malthusian argument that population is limited by food alone. It can also be used to demonstrate the need for conservation of capital resources.[1] If the goats had a little more power and intelligence they could build a

[1] See Sauvy, 1952.

fence, exclude the wolves, and multiply up to some maximum number.

But the optimum sized population for the goats is also the optimum sized population of goats from the point of view of the wolves—without the ring fence. For the wolves could maintain a larger population if there were a larger population of goats. Further, the wolves, if they were concerned for the future of their race as well as for the present, would eat such a number of goats as equalled the natural rate of increase of the goat population. If they ate up the whole of the goats as quickly as possible, they would be literally consuming their capital. But a similar argument could be applied by the goats, if they were not so silly, to the crops of grass. Some animal populations, it appears, move round an equilibrium point rather than settle at the point itself. This may be because the predators that live on, say, population A are related to the size of population A by a more than proportionately increasing function. The more of A there are the much better chance there is of B being propagated (e.g., if B's eggs are hatched in A's entrails). There will be an increase of A to the point where B propagates on a large scale, which will decimate A, so providing insufficient hosts for B, and the cycle will begin again.

Bacteria and minute organisms of many kinds are predators on the human race. It might happen that the vulnerability of that race was more than proportionately increased by some particular increase in its numbers, but of this there is no certain knowledge; in the present epoch, our predators are being fought back faster than they can increase themselves.

The law of life of the individual organism is inexorable. One organism in relation to all other organisms must be more dependent on them than they are on it. Hence it must follow the given law of growth and decline to an inevitable death. By an analogy, which seems applicable in all cases, any finite group of organisms is in the same case, if it is small in relation to the total population of partly rival organisms. But the analogy cannot be applied to life itself, nor to organisms that are capable of endless adaptations to the changing conditions of the universe; the laws of ecology do not predict a lifeless planet.

The human population is, however, mostly in a double relationship with other populations, because it is co-operative up to a point, and beyond that point competitive. This might be the relationship between the human population and cows, for example: LRR' representing the number of humans that could exist for the given number of cows on the Y-axis, and QRR' showing the corresponding schedule for the cow population (Diagram V). Up to R' the two populations are co-operative and above the line SRT the two populations will tend to move to stable equilibrium at R'. Populations of either cows or humans to the left of SRT (which is determined by the assumption of vector pull being equally proportionate to distance from the two curves) cannot exist; the vector lines will lead to the origin. Thus the minimum populations for cows and people are to the right of SRT, a point of unstable equilibrium occurring at R.

R' may be the highest point for both curves, which may each complete a rough semi-circle and return to its axis. In this eventuality R' is a maximum for both populations. This, however, implies two possible cow populations for any given human population and *vice versa*. Let the continuation of the human population curve back to the Y-axis be considered. From R'

onwards it is negatively inclined for humans, which means that the more cows there are above the critical number measured by IR' the less humans can survive. Finally, once OM cows exist humans become extinct. Beyond IR' cows are competitive, on balance, rather than co-operative, with humans.

In a period during which the stock of available agricultural land was fixed (or could only be increased at a critically slow rate), some such an interdependence as this might be a realistic restriction on numbers. If protein is essential for human life, and if protein can only be economically obtained from milk, milk products or meat, then an increase in the number of cattle will be essential, up to some point, determined partly by some other restriction, perhaps the necessity to reserve sufficient land for cereal production without which other essential food-stuffs would be insufficient. Beyond that point any extra head of cattle would serve to increase the protein available only at the heavy cost of reducing the bread supply, and so restricting the size that the population could attain. Commodities that are co-operative over one range and competitive over another may be quite common.

Man is an animal, and in a state of nature, if it so happened that his tendency to reproduce were uncontrolled, human populations would be limited in the same way as populations of animals and of plants. But men have civilized themselves and framed economic systems, which presumably means that they have done certain things which they thought would solve actual problems as they arose. The economic system, such as it is at any particular date, is in itself a protest against the working of blind ecological laws. The primitive men who decided to save seed for the next harvest were probably interfering with the laws of nature as then understood by the elders of the tribe.

Interference with the ecological restrictions on population (and on income per head) takes two forms, the organization of production, and the organization of consumption. Production is, in general, breaking through natural limitations to the increase of consumable or useful goods, attained by modifying the form of natural units of raw materials, and consumption is determined not only by what exists, and by what has been produced in the past, but by what is wanted now, and by existing social standards.

Production and demand functions thus constantly change the shape and significance of "natural" ecological relationships. The usual ecological laws depend upon the number of units of a population being functionally dependent on the existing size of that population, so that any given population will grow in favourable conditions; this is no longer true if production decisions can be taken. Similarly, the ecological laws rely on an unchanging need of one set of organisms for the use of others, but needs may change once the possibility of choice is admitted.

§ 5. *The Malthusian and Godwinian Results.* Neo-Malthusian theory concentrates on a relationship between size of population and supply of real income (or "food"), and on a constant demand per head for real income, at a minimum standard. There is, then, a functional dependence of population upon income in the form of subsistence, and diminishing returns are predicted. It follows that population will expand to some point at which the S curve has fallen to equality with the amount of produce indicated by the MSL straight line. (Oy is real income, or "food", OGS the total real product curve,

and MSL, the minimum standard of life, total demand.)
Neo-Malthusian theory equates population with ON_5
when all the forces at work have worked themselves out,
and population is back to its dreary subsistence standard
of life.

The neo-Godwinians assume, on the other hand, that
the rate of increase of population is a *decreasing* function
of an increasing standard of life (they usually think solely

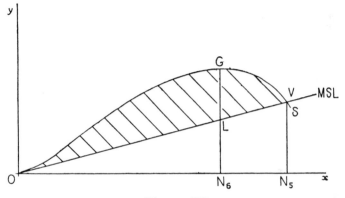

Diagram VI

in terms of natural increase, and of the decline in the
numbers of children per family as income per head
grows); thus, to them the decline in the birth-rate is a
function of the shaded area between the supply curve
and the MSL line. When this shaded area has reached
some critical level (either for individuals or for the community)—perhaps for the sake of argument when it
reaches the total of OGL—then population becomes
stationary at ON_6. This determines the future output of
the community.

CHAPTER VI

EQUILIBRIUM AND WORKING POPULATION

§ 1. *The Economic Demand for Labour.* Economic demand may not (or may) be entitled to reverential treatment,[1] but it may, quite neutrally, be recognized to be an important factor in determining the supply of most goods and services. A high demand for hand-painted ties has some effect on the supply of these goods; the mechanism linking supply to demand may be morally justifiable, within such restrictions as the state may rightfully impose, even though the objects produced in response to demand do not, by some æsthetic or moral standard, always seem to merit the price offered for them.

Demand affects the supply of human beings as well as of commodities and services; the connection exists, but its exact nature is not easy to discover.

High rewards for workers in a particular industry, persisting over a sufficient span of years, and not offset by some disadvantages of the work, will attract labour to that industry. But before a worker moves into a new industry he wants to know, of course, not only the ruling rate of wages, but the prospects of obtaining a job. The same principles may be supposed to apply to the longer-run demand for labour. A persistently high demand for labour, that is, the offer of *more* jobs at *higher* wages than before, will very likely increase the economic desirability to parents of having children, for one of two obvious reasons. The first, is that, especially for peasants or

[1] The "sovereignty of the consumer" is regarded as an ethical principle by some.

working-class people, children who earn money are a direct economic asset, and an insurance to their parents against misfortunes; and secondly, those classes of parents who do not look to see a financial return to themselves from their sons and daughters set as their target a standard of living for their potential offspring. The higher that standard the more likely they are to have some children, although evidently if there is an expensive training required, the number of children may be limited.

A "high" demand for labour will mean different things in different economic and social contexts. If children can be put to work at ten years of age they clearly become an economic asset to a working-class family much sooner than if they cannot leave school till they are sixteen. In those parts of Asia where the birth-rate is peculiarly high, children often work at even younger ages, and employment of a kind can always be found owing to the primitive social as well as economic conditions. Hence the high birth-rates there can be explained as partly due to the "high" demand for labour, although the wages and the jobs would not attract European juveniles. The very fact that the expectation of life is low (and that life is "cheap" per unit) means that a larger number of children is economically advantageous to the family.

No one can say how far fluctuations or trends in births are due to changes in parents' response to what they take to be the ruling (and future anticipated) economic demand for children. But that there is a considerable degree of connection can hardly be questioned. One part of the explanation of the falling birth-rate in Britain since 1870 may be found in the decline in the anticipated, and relative, net returns to be gained from children. In the 1860's it was possible for a working-man to expect some return from his children by the time that they were ten, a return that was high relative to his own wage and little reduced from a gross figure by the subtraction of the costs of upbringing and schooling.

The effect of the economic demand is not always easy to trace, because of the division of society into different social classes. The better-off classes, being leaders of social manners, have been handicapped in family-building by their recognition of the value (not all of it economic) of education and training. Setting themselves high ideals on these points, they have tended to restrict their families more drastically than other classes have done. Among their motives, anticipated economic advantage must have been important.

§ 2. *The Supply of Labour.* The supply of working-population comes from two sources, natural "increase" and net immigration (which may take negative values). To some extent, and sometimes by methods, such as infanticide and abortion, that are repugnant, individuals have always attempted to control fertility in most societies that have ever existed. The motives for these attempts have been numerous, but one major motive has undoubtedly been economic, and responsive to the changing labour market.

The control of fertility has been made progressively easier, as improved contraceptive devices have been invented, and knowledge of them made available. For economic reasons contraceptive practices are likely to be improved, and to be even more widely used. There are three ways, however, in which restrictions are likely to be imposed upon their universal adoption.

First, there is the old difficulty of the expense and effectiveness of any contraceptive device, however ingenious. The scientific problem is how to inhibit sperm from fertilizing any ovum, somewhere in the process of the chain of events during which semen makes its way to the uterus. There are weak links in the chain. Many possibilities are still being explored, such as inhibiting ovulation, controlling pituitary hormones, or developing an effective spermicide. (It has often been suggested that the decline in fertility which usually accompanies a rising standard of living is partly due to the more widespread use of soap, since soap is a very potent killer of sperms.)

Current methods of contraception cannot readily be used by men and women with a very low standard of living; there is always, in any society, a "residual group", whose habits are such that the use of *any* contraceptive would be too troublesome. In areas of very high fertility and low levels of living such groups may be significantly large, and substantial social changes will be a prerequisite of the wider use of contraception.[1] There must, after all, be a desire to limit family size, as well as a means of limiting it, and this desire is a function of the standard of living, and of the education and the morale of individuals.

But the difficulties in the way of the "residual" group using contraceptives apply only in slightly lesser degree for hundreds of thousands of peasant villages throughout the over-populated rural areas of India or Egypt, or for that matter Italy and South-East Europe. There has been discussion in the American scientific journals [2] of research work on an anti-fertility drug to be administered orally, which would obviate the disadvantages of existing devices, whether physical or chemical in their action. Even such an orally administered drug would have to be taken at the right time in the right quantity, and, unless some Government chose to subsidize it or distribute it free, its cost might not be negligible. While the perfection

[1] See Stix, 1941, p. 41. [2] E.g., *Science.*

II

of such a method might wipe out many of the present difficulties, there would still be social and economic problems to be solved before it could be used satisfactorily to control the high birth-rates of the world. The individual woman would have to desire family limitation sufficiently to put herself to the trouble and expense of taking the drug. Only in these conditions would it have an effect on birth-rates analogous to the spectacular effects of penicillin and sulpha drugs on the death-rates.

With these qualifications, the possibility of some rapid declines in birth-rates is undoubtedly opened up by the researches still in progress. It is, however, impossible to predict which birth-rates will decline the most; new inventions tend to be exploited much more rapidly in industrialized than in economically backward areas, and any such inventions, once available, might lead to a more rapid fall of birth-rates in Western Europe, which would precede the even steeper fall eventually due in Asiatic and African countries.

The second problem of control of fertility is the attitude of social and religious leaders. Many spokesmen for religions, like Malthus himself, advocate limitation of population only by the method of abstinence, austerity and self-control.

Other schools of moralists take the view that the use of contraceptives is ethically justified if the purpose for which they are employed is a good one. If they are employed to preserve and promote the health and happiness of the family they are justified; if only for the purpose of gratification of "illicit" sexual appetite, they are to be deprecated.[1]   Yet other writers, while affecting

[1] This was the point of view expounded by Dr. Sarvepalli Radhakrishnan, Vice-President of India, in his address to a conference on planned parenthood, November 11, 1952 (see *Eugenics Review*, Vol. 45, No. 1, April 1953, p. 15).

neutrality on the moral issues, believe quite simply that "people enjoy sex" and "are entitled to go on doing so".

The values of all societies are, however, changing, nor is the predominant or "official" ethos of any society either accepted, or its precepts followed, by even a majority of its members. As Professor Glass has remarked [1] contraception has been practised increasingly despite state and religious opposition. If it is accepted that increased concern for children by parents is a good thing, and that a high rate of infantile mortality is unavoidable without control of fertility, even believers in some of the religious arguments might accept control of fertility as the lesser of two evils.

The third point which affects control of fertility is the variation in sexual behaviour to be found from one society to another.[2] In man, as against other mammalian species, it appears that sexual behaviour is most easily affected by learning and by social conditioning. Nothing could be more false than the supposition that man's urge to procreate is an unchanging force unaffected by the society in which he lives.

The supply of human beings, economically considered, is a supply of labour. Some economic and social arrangements are conducive to a very rapid increase in population. In an island such as Mauritius, for example, the local demand for hands was exceptionally high in the nineteenth century, and the immigration of Indians to the sugar estates was encouraged. By 1910 government-assisted immigration ceased. Thereafter, a high, and since 1945 an enormous, rate of natural increase has occurred. How can this phenomenon be explained?

No doubt the detailed explanation would require a

[1] Glass, 1953.
[2] See, for example, Ford and Beach, 1952.

separate treatise; but the broad facts seem to be these. The social pressure of the Indians led to a breaking up of estates, which were divided and sold to former labourers in periods of low sugar prices. (The social structure of Mauritius approximated to that of the landholding society imagined by the earlier economists.) With the dividing of some of the estates total sugar production increased. Population over the last thirty years rose enormously, by 32 per cent, and agricultural production by 87 per cent; natural increase, though now at the high rate of 3 per cent per annum, has not outrun the basic output of crops.[1]

Thus, what might seem at first glance to be a case of a high birth-rate swamping any possibility of social advance is in fact a case of population breeding in response to the classic needs of first a plantation and then a peasant society, with a small dominant class of rentiers. The position, it is true, is by no means stable. A slump in sugar prices would cause a temporary disaster, as would hurricanes two years running. But these are hazards of any society, only perhaps more violent. Why has the birth-rate of the Indo-Mauritians not yet been controlled? Surely the answer largely lies in their social and economic state; with only a few children educated to secondary school level, out of a population of nearly 400,000, it is hardly surprising that the high quality small family pattern of living has not yet been adopted. Only when more skilled occupations are open to the Indo-Mauritians is a change in their desire to have large families to be expected.

This is only one example, and the argument does not rest on its validity alone. In every country of the world economic and social factors will be found to operate, and in most the economic will be the more important. In

[1] See *Mauritius, 1951*, H.M.S.O., 1952.

some places, no doubt, a demographic trend persists out of all reference to the current and future economic prospects of the country in which it occurs—just as Vienna could not rapidly re-adjust its population to the new circumstances decreed at the Treaty of Versailles. But in the long run, and despite some exceptions, economic circumstance is likely to be predominant.

Although no exact correspondence between children produced and labour required is likely to be found in any country of the world, and local variations will occur for the reasons suggested, it may be expected that supply will adjust itself to demand more readily as control of fertility is increased.

§ 3. *The Balance of Demand and Supply.* The demand for workers and the supply come towards some kind of balance. Evidently, on Marshallian lines of reasoning, the equilibrium need never be struck, but only be a point to which the economic system would tend if no further changes took place.

In several ways, however, supply and demand for workers are dependent on each other, both through the state of techniques and through the character of the institutional arrangements. This introduces several complications into the analogy of a simple mechanical equilibrium.

For the problem has to be thought of not in terms of finding sufficient food, but of finding the right proportions of all the commodities that need to be produced, and the right techniques of exchange as well as of production. The future of a population depends on these total solutions, not on partial solutions.

As Sir James Steuart wrote:

"We may lay it down as a principle, that a farmer

will not labour to produce a superfluity of grain relatively to his own consumption, unless he finds some
want which may be supplied by means of that superfluity; neither will other industrious persons work to
supply the wants of the farmer for any other reason
than to procure subsistence, which they cannot otherwise so easily obtain.　These are the reciprocal wants
which the statesman must create, in order to bind
society together."[1]

For population to increase there must, on Steuart's
principle, be a balanced development of industry as well
as of agriculture; a principle that is directly relevant to
the world population problem to-day.

Two fears haunt the economist, however, when he
reflects on the means of roughly preserving this balance
as population grows: first, the fear of diminishing returns,
and second, the fear of a failure in demand, giving rise
to unemployment whether originating *either* from technological labour-saving improvements *or* from institutional
shortcomings.

Fear number one can be summarily disposed of;
diminishing returns are not a bogey that ought to frighten
anyone capable of discerning the immense ranges of output in all industries, including agriculture, where increasing
returns are possible.[2]

For the second fear several anodynes have been applied.
The long-term worry is that as technological advance
takes place many workers will become redundant.　The
usual reply is that as wealth increases more needs can be
satisfied, and the displaced workers can enter into new,

[1] Steuart, 1767, Vol. i, p. 28.
[2] Cannan and Robbins pointed this out very firmly in the late 1920's.
Increasing returns are meant here both in the static and dynamic
senses.

or expanded, "secondary" or "tertiary" forms of employment.

Thus, in an advanced economy it would be likely that a relatively quite small proportion of workers would be found to be engaged directly in manufacturing, and a high proportion in the service or "tertiary" sections. One version of this theory has been well argued by Mr. Colin Clark who sought confirmation for it from statistics of distribution of working population in different countries, and certainly the high proportion of employed in "service" industries of all kinds in the U.S., the richest country in the world, seemed, together with some other facts, consistent with his suggested hypothesis that a high ratio of tertiary employment was a criterion of a country's wealth.

But primitive economies, as well as advanced, may have a high proportion of tertiary employment.[1]

Statistics are inconclusive, because in economies emerging from a primitive state nearly all adults and most children are engaged in trade whatever else they may be doing (and classified as doing) for their main occupation. Luxurious demands may promote primary employment (lobsters and furs), and necessitous demands may require manufactures or tertiary employment. There have to be some retailing and transport in all economies, and a high proportion in those progressing from tribal conditions.

One more point may be made on the contrast between the primitive and the advanced economy. Unemployment may be rife in a relatively primitive economy, but go unrecorded. There can be many unemployed under other names (beggars, landless peasants, part-time servants and so on); it is in the advanced economies that servants are difficult to get at the going wage, while in

[1] See Bauer and Yamey, 1951, and the rejoinder by Triantis, 1953.

the under-developed countries service is plentiful, this contrast showing better than statistics where under-employment is severest.

It is not, then, correct to think of economies advancing and "creating" an unemployment problem, which is then more or less adequately solved by a big increase in "tertiary" employment. This is a partial, and not a complete picture.

Let us begin again with definitions. Primary may be defined to include those activities directly concerned with winning results from the human environment, that is, in procuring raw materials or food, by processes directly linked with natural resources. This would include mining, fishing, most agriculture, wood-felling and so on; but not diamond-polishing, fish manure preparation, butter-making or carpentry, which would be in the secondary group. The secondary group covers all manufacturing and preparation of goods up to the stage of a wholesale sale. The tertiary group covers the rest: that is, every kind of service and clerical and administrative work. Thus the classification is inevitably occupational and not industrial, and relates *both* to the stage of production reached, from the raw material to the finished product, *and* to the nature of the activity whereby production is assisted.

A study of the growth of the American economy certainly reveals a high proportion of tertiary types of employment which it has been able to support out of its reserves and surpluses of spending-power. But pheno-menal as America's transport, commercial, advertising and beauty parlour types of employment are, its main-tenance of primary production at a high level is also significant.

One fallacy that has been committed by some is the

identification ¹ of primary types of employment with diminishing, secondary with increasing, and tertiary with constant returns.

The essential point lies in Steuart's phrase that "the statesman must create" reciprocal wants. For an increased population to be supported two conditions are necessary. First, a sufficient economic surplus must be available to meet more than the current needs of the existing adult members of the population. Second, that surplus (and the flow of purchasing-power generally) must be channelled into directions which keep the increased population usefully employed, but there seem to be no good grounds for supposing that a growing economic surplus necessarily results in an increasing percentage of tertiary (or any other particular type of) employment. America is not necessarily the archetype of progressive economies, but an economy which progressed in very special circumstances. In Canada, where somewhat similar circumstances prevail, a similar pattern may be followed. In Britain, on the other hand, there are good reasons for supposing that the danger is that real incomes will be kept down by a failure to shift enough resources into secondary employment, and to keep down the level of tertiary employment, which tends to rise particularly under conditions of an increasing degree of monopoly in industry. In India, and the other heavily populated areas of the world, now embarking on industrialization, a different policy again may be appropriate, but, whatever the conditions, the object of policy is not to increase one or other sector of employment for its own sake, but to provide those types of employment that are most

¹ Professor Sauvy expressly introduced this identification as a hypothesis; but some other writers wrongly assume the identification to be both self-evident and true.

productive in the light of the special economic conditions of the particular country.

As Sauvy has argued, if the seigneurs of a landlord-dominated society take the decision to spend their rents not on employing musicians and grooms but on some goods requiring little labour, some of a previously balanced population becomes wholly redundant. *Mutatis mutandis*, in any society strategic decisions are constantly being taken which may raise or lower the demand for labour. One set of decisions would use increased real incomes to keep labour demand high, and another set might weaken that demand, and would be reflected in a tendency for the rate of emigration to increase.

The statesman may "create" reciprocal wants, in favourable circumstances, by adopting a policy of *laissez-faire*, because he expects that the price mechanism alone will result in the necessary expansion of tertiary employment, and other employment, to take up any slack caused by technological change. But in other circumstances the only ways to keep the population employed may require state planning.

Present knowledge of industrial techniques, and of ways of living, has run so far ahead of average performance that it is difficult to believe that most western countries are too thickly populated. With the necessary guidance on investment and development their working populations could probably in most cases increase, and at the same time enjoy better living.

CHAPTER VII

THE EXPANDING ECONOMY

Two subjects remain to be discussed: whether the conclusions of the last chapters are altered because capital
is liable to be too scarce to support population, and,
secondly, whether the rates of change of population are
liable to be inconsistent with the optimum, or even the
possible, rates of expansion of the different parts of the
world economy.

§ 1. *Capital per Head of Population.* One way of defining
the optimum population would be in terms of capital
per head, and another in terms of land per head.

One argument that had a certain plausibility in the
period 1946–50 ran as follows: first, in general terms, any
country which had more real capital per worker than it
had before would *ipso facto* be better off, "real capital"
being defined as "stock of machines and industrial equipment". *Ergo*, any industrial country would be better
off, so far as the static analysis went, if it had a smaller
population than that which it had at present. Secondly,
a smaller population than the existing one (whatever it
is) would allow more house-room per head of population.
Ergo, a reduction in population would increase economic
welfare.

If these two arguments are accepted, then, apart from
any qualifications due to the fact that *changes* in population may be harmful, it must be concluded that every
country of the world is over-populated. Furthermore,
so far as this static argument is concerned, every

country in the world that contains a greater population than one individual is over-populated. That one person, if all the others vanished, would have an enormous volume of capital, and unlimited house-room. (He would not even have to work, as he could live out his life on stored foodstuffs.)

The protagonists of this theory of over-population do not push their argument quite so far as this, since they usually admit that, while a reduction in the size of the population of almost any area must on their theory be beneficial, such a reduction must not be carried to the point where any substantial advantages of large-scale production are lost. But, on their view, losses of this kind are trifling for a considerable range; so they come back to the contention that quite large reductions of population would in most countries be beneficial. The argument proves a great deal too much, as has been shown by the *reductio ad absurdum*. Why is it necessarily fallacious?

The criterion of "capital per head" in determining the optimum requires very much closer examination. It is true that workers in manufacturing in Europe as compared with the United States have less capital equipment per head, and that this often seems to be the reason for a sustained overall relatively low level of labour productivity which depresses the standard of life. But there are many steps to take before it can be argued that an increased capital per head would have the result (even on static assumptions) of raising real net incomes; such factors as the size of the markets secured, and the cost of the capital to be introduced, are two well-known additional considerations.

If the argument in favour of a reduced population assumes that the type of capital remains unchanged, then of course it falls to the ground immediately. A reduction in the number of workers would in that case most probably result in redundancy of machines. The argument must then assume that the stock of capital equipment is adjusted to the new smaller size of working population.

A high amount of capital goods per worker is not in itself advantageous. On the contrary, if there is a given stock of capital in a country (its form being assumed flexible) then, up to some critical point, the greater the population the better; in other words, the *less*, overall, the capital per worker the better off each of them will be per head. Supposing the capital invested in a new town amounts to £100 millions, to cover all buildings, services and equipment. Up to some critical point, at which substantial disadvantages accrue, the more the people using that equipment the lower the cost per head. But this applies if the equipment cost £10 only and not £100 millions. It is an advantage that accrues from spreading an initial capital cost, and has little to do with what is usually thought of under the heading "advantages of large-scale production".

At any given time, the capital equipment of a country is limited, and has had a definite economic cost; the greater the use that can be made of that equipment before it wears out, the lower the cost per head. It is true that if the country suddenly and instantaneously lost some population there would be more capital per head left to use, and as that capital would have already been produced it would be temporarily treated as cost-less, a windfall to the new (smaller) population. But from this arid proposition nothing can be deduced as to whether the country is, or is not, over-populated.

A more fruitful way of looking at population in relation

to capital equipment is to allow first for the cost of that equipment, secondly for the nature of the equipment, and thirdly for the employment opportunities in the community as a whole. If all these have certain assumed values, then it is possible to consider what size of population is "optimum" (say, in terms of greatest possible *net* output per head) for a given quantity of capital. A reduction in the size of population below that optimum figure, whatever it is, would be harmful on this criterion, and not beneficial just because it was a reduction in numbers.

This approach has a special application to the understanding of the phenomenon of increasing urbanization. Much more social and other capital is to be found in cities than in rural districts; the agriculturist, moreover, usually appears in this country to be working in conjunction with a rather low quantity of working capital and building investment. It might thus be supposed that towns were places of relatively high capital per head, and the country a place of low capital per head. But this is sometimes an illusion. For the greater capital of the towns is in constant use by a far denser population. The population density of the city, especially in the day-time, may be several thousand times the density of an extensive rural district. The latter has its roads and railways, but these, even if inferior, are used by far fewer people than the city streets and metropolitan railways. If all the facts were available it might well work out that in some cases the country districts were served by more capital per head than the towns and cities; the overall productivity of the country would be lower, relating value of output to cost, just because of this unavoidable over-capitalization.

The trend towards urbanization can thus be seen as a

method of taking advantage of capital equipment. Over time and with technical change, this means securing more capital per head; but, at a given time, and with a limited quantity of equipment, the whole point of urbanization is to secure less capital per head. A static analysis does not therefore permit of the fallacious conclusion that any population may always become individually richer by reducing its numbers.

Some special kinds of "capital goods" are of particular importance; the rise of industrial civilization has taken place *pari passu* with an increased use of motive power; real incomes have increased as horse-power used per head has increased. The expansion of power use per head depends on the consumption of fuels. This raises the special "bottleneck" problem of the possible rate of expansion of fuel supplies (oil, coal, water-power and atomic energy), but as will be seen in a later chapter, this problem does not seem likely to be incapable of solution over the next half-century.

§ 2. *Economic Growth*. The neo-classical (Marshallian) answer to the problem of population [1] was that organization as well as invention would result in a "law of increasing return" that would offset any tendency for "diminishing returns" to set in. Thus Marshall wrote that "an increase of labour and capital leads generally to improved organization, which increases the efficiency of labour and capital", and this is, indeed, his "law of increasing returns", as distinct from any consequence of new techniques and inventions. Such improved organization was the result of a greater scale of activity (or could only be achieved *with* a greater scale of activity). "In a

[1] At first posed by Malthus, and then changed into a different form by Ricardo and Mill.

larger scale of production, which is the main feature of higher organization, the layout may, by mere concentration, require less than twice the material of machinery and building, as well as of fuels in order to double the output of the establishment. This is not technique, or new powers of machinery, but simply economy of size." [1]

Such economies of size may spread from one establishment to another, or occur as the result of the simultaneous growth of different industries. In this case they are called by the neo-classicists "external" economies. All this sounds as though the changes might be gradual, "at a more regular pace", as Professor McGregor puts it, than the introduction of inventions and discoveries. But such changes of scale *may* have results as sudden, discontinuous and spectacular as that of a new product like the internal combustion motor engine. A dynamic, and by no means necessarily gradual, increase in output per head may be the direct consequence of an improved organization made available when economies of scale are realized. Ever since Marshall's time this important principle has been known, but its effective application to the analysis of dynamic situations has not been made.

Dynamic economics must take account not only of steady change but of the consequence of shocks due to innovations, and to developments in organization, which affect the structure of economic life. [2]

One of the clearest and most widely discussed state-

[1] McGregor, 1949, p. 20.
[2] Professor Samuelson has pointed out an important danger in dynamic process analysis: "The number of conceivable models is literally infinite and a life-time may be spent in exploring possibilities" (see *A Survey of Contemporary Economics*, ed. H. S. Ellis, 1948, p. 375). The only safeguard is to confine attention to those (possible) sequences of development which, by an act of possibly unscientific judgment, are deemed the most interesting or likely.

ments of a stagnationist theory has been that put forward by Professor Hansen in 1939. He was writing of the long-period, that is, of the change of population over decades. America, he thought, faced an ultimate contraction in numbers, and an immediate decline in its rate of growth.[1] Hansen regarded it as "an indisputable fact" that the prevailing economic system of capitalism had never been able to reach reasonably full employment, or the attainment of its currently realizable maximum real income, without very large investment expenditures. He harked back to Wicksell's view that the operative factor[2] was the prospective rate of profit on new investment. Now this rate of profit had in the past been geared largely to the rate of population growth.

Hansen estimated that of the approximate 3 per cent per annum growth of physical output in Western Europe (4 per cent in the U.S.A.) over a long period, rather less than half might have been attributed to population growth in Western Europe, and a little over half to the same cause in the U.S.A. Thus, very roughly, 40 per cent of capital formation in Western Europe and 60 per cent in the U.S.A. was ascribed by Hansen to population growth.

Since this source of demand for capital, and of labour supply to provide capital goods, was drying up, Hansen predicted that to maintain full employment more and more reliance would have to be placed upon technological developments, and the consequent demand for new investment.

The stagnationists' case originally rested partly on the assertion that there has been a widening of capital and no

---

[1] From an increase of 16 millions in the 1920's to 8 millions in the 1930's, and perhaps $5\frac{1}{2}$ millions in the 1940's according to the forecasts then acceptable (actual increase in the 1940's was 16 millions).

[2] "Active, dominant and controlling factor" was Hansen's phrase.

(net) deepening;[1] but if economies of scale can be proved to have resulted from increased population, then a slower rate of growth will reduce the rate at which such advantages can be realized. It is, unfortunately, difficult to give any quantitative measure of economies of scale, but this does not mean that they are unimportant. If they are important, a cessation of population growth could result in symptoms of stagnation, whatever the trend in the relative proportions of "widened" and "deepened" capital formation.

For example, the cost of retailing, the cost of house-building, the cost of long-distance passenger transport and the cost of entertainment are all substantially less for the urban dweller in Great Britain than for the dweller in a small town or a remote country district. One reason for the persistent trend towards city-building the world over is that closely packed mass-markets are the only markets than can be relatively cheaply provided with shops, dwellings, railway services and amusements. Public services such as drainage, water and electricity and gas can also be laid on economically only for certain minimum concentrations of population, though these services (like the others) may rise sharply in cost if the demand is excessive.

Much smaller though it has been, the recovery in the output of Britain from 1946 to 1950, and of Germany from 1949 to 1952, shows the extraordinary reserves of modern industrial civilization and its powers of adaptation and change.

---

[1] Hansen went so far as to assert in 1939 that "our system of production is little more capitalistic than fifty or seventy-five years ago. It requires, in other words, a period of employment of our productive resources no longer than formerly to reproduce the total capital stock. . . ." He thought that ". . . now with the rapid cessation of population growth, even the widening process may slow down."

The stagnationists' analysis of the rôle played by population in the economic growth of the community was perhaps too much over-simplified.   They emphasized just *one* functional relationship, the alleged dependence of a high proportion of real annual investment upon the rate of growth of the population of a country.   Thus they overlooked, or deliberately ignored, the many possible variants of this relationship, or the cross-relationships that might exist (for example, that population might be itself stimulated to growth if, as the result of some external stimulus, the real national income increased rapidly).   The stagnationists, of whom Keynes himself was perhaps the least dogmatic, emphasized the Keynesian danger of insufficient investment, and wrote this into the long-term as well as the short-term prognostication of our economic ills.

The late Professor Schumpeter, on the other hand, once remarked that :

"By 'growth' we mean changes in economic data which occur continuously in the sense that increment or decrement per unit of time can be currently absorbed by the system without perceptible disturbance.   Increase of population, resulting in an increase of the supply of labour of at most a few per cent per year (historically an increase of three per cent is already high), is the outstanding example." [1]

Schumpeter explicitly brought out a hidden assumption of many theorists, namely, that the influence of population was numerically so small as to be capable of being "currently absorbed" by a progressive economic system without much evidence of a shock effect.   He himself

[1] "Analysis of Economic Change", *Review of Economic Statistics,* Vol. XVII, No. 4, May 1935, reprinted in *Readings*, etc., 1950.

proceeded to emphasize the much greater importance of major technical "innovations".

Most studies of economic growth have so far been concentrated upon problems of disturbance, that is, upon cyclical questions. This approach has no doubt been due to, and partly justified by, the fact that, apart from major political events like war, the trade cycle has been the major economic event of the last thirty years.

Many models of an expanding economy owe their origin, as Mrs. Robinson has pointed out,[1] "to a simple piece of arithmetic". What they attempt to establish is the existence of a "growth rate" which fulfils certain conditions. For example, if one condition is that the stock of capital in a country has a fixed relation to income (capital is n times income), and another condition is that r per cent of income is saved and used in net investment (net additions to capital stock), then "the piece of arithmetic" tells us that there is a growth rate of r/n per cent which, if followed, would enable these conditions to be fulfilled indefinitely. For $n =$ capital $\div$ income, and $r =$ investment in the year $\div$ income ($\times 100$), so clearly $r \div n$ = investment as a percentage of capital stock; i.e., the growth rate of capital stock. But income is a fixed fraction of capital stock by condition one, and investment is a fixed fraction of income. So income, too, must expand at this growth rate. So must investment, and so, incidentally, must consumption.

This, indeed, is always the basic point of the model, dressed up though it may be to give emphasis to quite different applications. On the assumptions of the model, the economy must continually expand at a pre-determined rate and so must both investment and consumption. Granted the conditions, then, attention is focused on any

[1] Robinson, J., 1952.

difficulties that may arise in the way of maintaining the necessary rate of advance.

Some authors, considering the long-term problems, have worried themselves about the possibility of finding sufficient investment opportunities, others have concerned themselves with the difficulty of expanding consumption, and still others with the possibility of maintaining the required supply of capital goods. Some have used the model to prove that the economy *could* expand, others to show that it was almost certain not to be able to keep up the pace. Very few have related the problem in any specific way to the problems of an expanding (or declining) population.

But the main fear of the model-makers has been of population as a *limiting factor of supply* (a "ceiling") rather than as a limiting factor of demand (as in the literature of the 1930's). Perhaps this concern with a possible shortage of man-power to support an expanding economy is a sign of the times, and illustrates the tacit recognition of the great potential wealth per head in the world believed to be available to an increasing working population in a still growing industrial economy.

No economist can prove by *a priori* reasoning either the stagnationists' thesis or the theory that a limited man-power ceiling is the typical cause of cyclical fluctuations, nor has an empirical approach yet succeeded in yielding definitive results. It can be said, empirically, that population increase and industrial development have, in the last two hundred years, usually gone together. A society can be imagined in which strategic decisions were taken such that all increases in the economic surplus were devoted to raising the standard of living of the existing number of inhabitants, and an increase in numbers was kept rigidly at zero. But experience shows that the momentum of industrial development has more usually hitherto brought increases in numbers far above even the present natural rate of increase. A few countries, like France, have advanced industrially without much increase in population, but their rate of advance has been noticeably slower than that of their more rapidly industrializing neighbours. The same forces are likely to prevail in the future. Britain's economic survival in a competitive world surely implies some continued rise in population, so far as the present arguments provide any guide.

CHAPTER VIII

INTERNATIONAL MIGRATION

§ 1. *Types of Migration.* Migration is of two kinds: international, and that which takes place within the boundaries of a country or political unit. It will be convenient to adhere to this conventional dichotomy, although the distinction becomes difficult to maintain as meaningful in periods of fluctuating political boundaries. Ever since the eighteenth century boundaries have frequently been changed in all the continents. In the nineteenth century the United States of America extended its boundaries to include territories which are now inhabited by some 92 million persons; and in the period from 1939 to 1946 the U.S.S.R. extended its boundaries to include territories inhabited in 1939 by 18 million persons.[1] The United Kingdom reduced its boundaries after World War I, when it ceded independence to Southern Ireland.

Thus, what might have been an "internal" movement at one date is regarded as an "international" movement at another. It is evident, too, that the shifting of boundaries, itself a political event, sometimes follows and sometimes precedes a significant shifting of population from place to place.

So far as Britain is concerned "international" migration is usually identified with trans-oceanic migration, of a permanent or semi-permanent kind, for obvious geographical and historical reasons; while "internal" migration has traditionally been sometimes permanent and

[1] *Economic Bulletin for Europe,* Vol. I, No. 1, July 1949, U.N., Geneva, p. 11.

sometimes temporary or seasonal. Even the "internal" migration has given rise, however, to distinctly "nationalistic" problems, since the net flow has been so marked from Ireland, Wales and Scotland into the English (and Scottish) growing conurbations.[1] Internal migration has been both long-term, following certain trends, short-term, especially in times of war, and cyclical, such as the exodus from the depressed areas; and, although movements of males have been important, the characteristic of internal migration, especially in the nineteenth century, has been the predominance of females among migrants.[2]

The present chapter is confined to problems of international migration. As has already been seen, forecasts of population change made in the last twenty years have paid little attention to the possibility of extensive net migration from country to country. This omission has been defended on the grounds that the scale and direction of migration are *especially* difficult to predict. It must be conceded that guesses as to the future trend of events must, in this, as in other social and economic matters, be subject to a very high degree of uncertainty. But the special degree of uncertainty in regard to migration appears, on examination, to consist merely of the fact that a single change of policy (say a government's decision freely to admit Japanese or Italian migrants within its borders) may have rather large-scale consequences. This may affect the detailed timing of future migratory flows, but the broad picture of the future is perhaps no more uncertain than that which can be formed of other economic developments, and its accuracy will partly depend on how closely past trends can be analysed, and in particular

[1] The "gross" flow was offset by considerable counter-movements in the opposite direction.
[2] See Ravenstein, 1885.

upon how far the interconnections between demographic,
economic and political forces can be discerned.

§ 2. *Long-term, Permanent International Migration.*   There
are three further reasons why the importance of migration
for the future of the British and American (not to mention
other) populations has often been played down; one is
the widely held view that the nineteenth century was the
age *par excellence* of mass trans-oceanic movement of
population; second is the belief that high birth-rates,
producing a demographic "surplus population" are necessary as a push to Europeans to go overseas; and third is
the belief that unpredictable political barriers will always
prevent mass movements.

First, the simple fact is that migration has been proportionately, and lately even absolutely, as important for
Britain and America in the twentieth century as it was
in the nineteenth.   For example, the gross shifts of population, both in Europe and in the sub-continent of India,
from 1939 to 1949 exceeded in scale any mass movements
that have ever taken place before in ten years of recorded
human history.   Excluding the movements of slave
labour in the war years, it seems that at least 10 million
persons moved permanently from country to country in
the years 1946 and 1947 in Eastern Europe, following the
readjustments of frontiers.   There were enormous movements of population into and out of France.   The United
Kingdom received an inflow of 500,000 persons from 1939
to 1945, followed by an outflow in the years 1946 and
1947 of some 400,000.[1]

There is a tendency to discount the importance of these
movements as being partly forced or political in origin, and
as partly cancelling each other out (so far as they affect

[1] *Economic Bulletin*, cited above, July 1949, p. 17

total numbers). This last point is valid,[1] and war-time shifts of population are exceptional. But their net final effect is not negligible; nor have politically determined movements ceased to operate in the 1950's. It is as well to recall that nineteenth-century movements of population were also, if in less degree, partly forced and partly political in origin and not wholly spontaneous movements.

Looked back on from a distance, nineteenth-century international migration may seem part of a fairly rational process (with population flowing from less promising economies to those where more opportunity lay), not induced by inexorable political pressures nor giving rise to inhumane consequences. As many historians have pointed out, this was not how the movement always appeared to contemporary observers of, or participants in, it; very few migrants at any period can have suffered the upheaval of moving home, and of finding new ties, without some hardships before their departure, during their transit or after their arrival. Descriptions of the shiploads of Irish immigrants arriving at Quebec or Montreal in the 1850's do not make pleasant reading. The great bulges in the immigration curves represent periods of intense human misery.

The great migratory peoples of the world in the last two hundred years have been the Europeans, the Indians, the Chinese and Japanese and the Africans. The last group was moved to America under obvious duress, but some degree of compulsion has affected other parts of the great migratory flows. Economic push or pull seem, how-

---

[1] *Net* population shifts resulted, for example, in a gain to Germany, Austria and Italy of nearly 3 million persons from 1939–45, a gross inflow of 7·8 millions being offset by an outflow of 4·8 millions; in the years 1946–7 these countries gained by population shift another 7 million persons.

ever, to have been the main causes of the great majority of individual "free" movements.

The main outlines of the outward European movement are so well known that they need to be only briefly recapitulated. The biggest proportion of it consisted of emigration to the United States of America; total gross immigration to that country was put at 38 millions for the 110 years from 1820 to 1930,[1] of whom 26 millions are estimated to have stayed, and so added (in their lifetimes) to the population.

The gross number of passengers leaving the British Isles for extra-European destinations over the same period was some 20 millions, which can be taken as roughly equivalent to gross emigration. Net emigration was much less than this, owing to the steady backflow of earlier emigrants, and the influx of persons from other countries to live in Britain or to stay there preparatory to a further journey westwards. A great deal of British emigration (and of foreigners *via* Britain) was destined for various parts of the British Commonwealth. A very high proportion of Canada's army in World War I had been born in Britain.

According to a table published in 1924[2] of the 36 million "immigrants" to (passengers arriving in) the United States from 1820 to 1924, 24 per cent ($8\frac{1}{2}$ millions) came from the United Kingdom, 16 per cent from Germany, and 9 per cent from other parts of northern and western Europe; 13 per cent were from Italy, 12 per cent from Austria-Hungary, and 24 per cent from other parts of eastern and southern Europe. British North America and South America provided nearly 10 per cent, the remainder coming from China, India and Japan and other specified or unspecified countries of origin.

---

[1] Willcox, 1931, Vol. II, p. 89.
[2] In the *Monthly Labor Review*, Washington, January 1924.

The countries of origin of American immigrants changed considerably between the periods 1870–90 and 1900–13. In the first period roughly 75 per cent of immigrants were coming from the so-called "old" elements (i.e., from Britain, Scandinavia and Germany in the main), whereas from 1900 to 1913 nearly 75 per cent of the immigrants were "new" (i.e., from Turkey in Asia and southern Europe, especially Italy). America's peak year for "passengers entering" ended June 30, 1907, and in that year 1,285,000 such passengers were recorded; and in another high year ending June 30, 1914, there was an almost equally large number of entrants.

These high figures of inflow into America corresponded with an urgent pressure on population to leave Europe. This pressure had notably shifted from country to country.

Thus, in the 1850's, "British" (i.e., mainly Irish) emigrants had predominated, soon followed by German and Scandinavian. In 1891–95 emigrants from the British Isles still accounted for 20 per cent of the immigration into the United States, while Italy, Austria-Hungary and Russia each accounted for some 12 or 13 per cent. By 1906–10 Austria-Hungary accounted for 24 per cent of the immigrants, Italy for 22 per cent, and Russia for 20 per cent.[1]

In the light of these past events the break in the trends of trans-Atlantic migration that followed World War I assume a special meaning and importance. Three major changes took place: the introduction of the quota system by American legislation, the economic depression of the 1920's in Commonwealth countries, followed by the Great Depression of 1929–32, and the ban on Russian emigration that was enforced by the Soviet revolutionary government.

[1] Ferenczi, 1929, Vol. I, p. 179.

The "natural" or "normal" tendency of migratory flow seemed, up to the period 1920-32, when all these trends were reversed or interrupted by policy, to have followed a regular and intelligible development. Just as in the days of British free trade (which also ended in 1932) Great Britain was the "market of last resort", the market where goods could always be offered for sale by citizens of any country that was short of gold or liquid reserves, so, up to that same turning-point, the United States had been the country of last resort for the family forced to consider the grim prospects of unemployment, or near-starvation, or both, at home. Inevitably the Irish turned to America when in their crisis, as did the surplus workers from England, or the redundant Italians and Austrians; so, too, did the Russians as their economy in turn began to undergo some noticeable modernization. But these huge inflows of immigrants to America had caused immense social and political problems there, and the consequence was a momentous decision to cut down the inflow rather than to tackle the problems themselves.

What were the fundamental causes of the break in the mass trans-oceanic migration of the nineteenth century (actually of the early twentieth century as well, since it persisted at least until 1914)? Were they political, economic or demographic?

Political, certainly; for the American immigration restrictions were imposed as the result of a political agitation in America, brought to a head by the short-term economic problems of demobilization and of an agriculture excessively expanded for war needs. Restrictions on emigration were also political in origin. The Empire Settlement Act of 1922, under which by 1937 400,000 British nationals had been assisted to emigrate to Australia, Canada and New Zealand, was a politically conditioned measure. But movements on a much larger scale were intended when the Act was passed. Economic forces began to operate that put an effective end to the scheme.

Economic forces became clearly paramount, indeed, with the onset of the Great Depression. A net return movement to Europe, and especially to Britain, set in from 1931. This was a short-term effect. A more long-term economic force was the decline of the "open spaces" available for raising food by extensive agriculture overseas.

Demographic changes also played their part. There were the checks to population caused by the casualties, and fall of births, of World War I; and the perhaps more serious check to population growth in Western Europe caused by the decline in the average size of family. It has thus been argued that "from the merely demographic point of view there was certainly no surplus population available in most countries of north-western and central Europe" to provide for large-scale emigration in the period between the two world wars.[1]

The three types of forces must not be regarded as acting in isolation each from the other, nor must exaggerated importance be ascribed to any one of them. Political barriers, important though they are, can rarely be effective if put across the path of some really powerful economic drive. Permanent migration need not be trans-oceanic, which is relatively easy to control (although now by-passed sometimes by air traffic), but across land frontiers. In decades when the economic need for immigrants is great, short-term influxes of labour can rarely be wholly checked (witness the movements into the U.S. across the Canadian and Mexican frontiers, or into France from Italy

[1] Isaac, 1951, p. 190.

and Spain), and these eventually may lead to permanent settlement.

Economic forces are, in this connection, sometimes treated in an over-simplified way. It is argued that the main cause of the success of earlier permanent migration was that agriculture was being expanded overseas, providing cheap food for the manufacturing nations of Europe. The economic development was, then, complementary up to 1914, and thereafter the same opportunities no longer existed.

There is a recognizable truth in this well-known interpretation of events; but certain comments on it are required. First of all, it is a telescoping of events to imagine that a major part of the inflow into the United States in the fifty years before 1914 went into an expanding agriculture. The great bulk of the mass immigration went to build up a great new urban civilization, which to this day is for the greater part concentrated in the Eastern and Middle Western sections of the country.

Secondly, the long-term economic factors favourable to inward migration seem to have had less to do with the question of the agricultural/non-agricultural balance than with such structural questions as in which decades the railroads were due to be built, or the road system of the country reorganized; or with the possibility of changing techniques in which capital equipment could be used more and more by unskilled labour; or with opportunities for exploiting the economies of the division of labour (*either* within large *or* between multitudes of small plants).

Thirdly, there is the question of the organization of the capital markets at home and abroad. A certain structure of market at home might have acted as a deterrent to employment, since capital equipment at home could not be provided fast enough to keep all the available labour employed at a reasonable level of productivity. More persons, therefore, may have emigrated than otherwise would have done, and than were strictly necessary to increase agricultural output overseas.

Large-scale permanent international migration from Europe was resumed after World War II. Nearly 3 million persons emigrated from Europe to countries overseas in the five years after the end of the war, a figure to be compared with the $3\frac{1}{2}$ million moving overseas in the years 1920–24 inclusive.[1] This was nearly $4\frac{1}{2}$ times as many as left Europe in the five years preceding World War II.

Many of the factors favourable to migration could be classed as "short-term political", although some were economic. There were separated families and war brides (125,000 of them), political uncertainty at home, displaced persons from Germany with no homes left to return to, the millions of "expellees" of German ethnic origin, returning prisoners of war of various nationalities, Jews seeking their new national home, all these being politically determined. Emigration from Italy and the Netherlands was officially encouraged on economic grounds, that is, because these economies could not be adjusted to employ their fairly rapidly growing populations.

In the receiving countries economic conditions mainly determined the "pull" factors. The exceptionally full employment conditions ruling in the United States, for example, enabled that country to receive 216,000 displaced persons and 96,000 alien wives and fiancées of members of their armed forces by 1951, in addition to normal intake of immigrants under the Quota Act. Australia planned at first to receive 200,000 immigrants a

[1] *Ibid.*, 1952, p. 191.   The U.S. Quota Act was passed in 1924.

year by 1950, which proved impossible, and by 1952 the target had been reduced to 80,000.[1]

Several difficulties had to be overcome in the realization of this huge programme of emigration, the greater part of which was carried out by a body called the International Refugee Organization.[2]   There were the physical obstacles, such as shortage of shipping-space, and the arrears of house-building in the receiving countries, and social obstacles, such as the problem of reconciling Yorkshire miners to working side by side with Italians. Despite all the difficulties, some of which could not be solved, there was an exceptional tide of overseas migration, the International Labour Office estimate of 1951 being that some 5 million persons in Europe would be "available for migration" over the next five years, at least 4½ millions of them consisting of Italians and Germans.   Whether this estimate was accurate or not, on any reckoning the figure of persons so available must have been high.

How is the post-World War II wave of "permanent" migration from Europe to be regarded?   Was it solely a short-term politically determined phenomenon?   Or was it the resuming of an economically, and demographically, determined long-term trend?

From one point of view the movement was simply the aftermath of the war, an unravelling of the knots into which the Nazi regime had tied Europe.   But why had these knots been tied?   Simply because the Nazis had implemented on a colossal scale a manpower plan for European industry as a whole.   The consequence of that plan was forced international migration of a hitherto unprecedented magnitude.

[1] *Ibid.*, 1952, p. 194.
[2] See Isaac, 1952, and *Economic Bulletin for Europe*, Vol. I, No. 1, 1949.

A production plan for Europe as a whole, or for the
N.A.T.O. powers as a whole, indeed for any international
organization, necessarily involves a corresponding plan
for manpower. A manpower plan is likely to need, at
some stage, transfers of population from one country to
another. If the next fifty years are to see increasing
international economic planning in Western Europe, or
in Europe and the Atlantic Powers together with the
British Commonwealth, then it is likely that some attention will be given by the planning body to the problem of
moving population to the places where it is economically
most urgently needed. To discuss the future of population movements from Western Europe is to discuss the
future of international economic planning, without which
such movements are not likely to be very large.

In the 1920's and 1930's large-scale immigration of
Indians and Chinese into the Malayan Straits Settlements
took place, of the order of 300,000–400,000 persons a year.
But in more recent years the Indian and Chinese population there has tended to grow by natural increase rather
than by immigration. The late nineteenth- and early
twentieth-century immigration of Indians into Ceylon
had almost ceased by 1939, and there has been a noticeable back-flow of Indian immigrants to India, and an even
more marked back-flow from Burma.[1] The era of large-
scale international movements lasted longer in the East
than in the West, but increasing barriers have now slowed
down the movements there, at least temporarily; internal
migration in Eastern countries is now proceeding at a
very high rate. The rate of urbanization (i.e., population gains of cities from rural areas) in Japan exceeded

[1] See "International migrations in the Far East during recent times
—The countries of immigration", *Population Bulletin*, No. 2, October
1952, p. 27

the increase in its population from 1920 to 1940, and the rate of gain of Indian cities (some 1 million a year) is impressive.[1]

There are often thought to be three obstacles to large-scale mass emigration of the old style in modern conditions. The first two obstacles are real; the third partly illusory. The first is the actual physical difficulty of transfer, now that the shocking hygienic conditions of old-time migration are no longer tolerated. Ships have to be found, and passages paid for. (This is not, of course, a difficulty in the way of migration across land frontiers.) The second is the question of providing capital in the receiving country to house the immigrant and put him to work. The capital required per worker varies from country to country, and according to the occupation to be followed by the immigrant, but the sum needed is nowadays usually large, equal to the whole value of the new worker's output for a number of years. "Adequate" housing (i.e., of a standard that he will accept) can only be provided for the immigrant with great difficulty, if, as is often the case, housing is short for the existing inhabitants of the country.

In the nineteenth century land was "plentiful" in the U.S. and Canada, and scarce in the U.K.; and *both* labour *and* industrial capacity (and social capital) were relatively scarce to land in the U.S. and Canada.

The mass of immigrants could in the long run build capital equipment as well as raise food; and the problem of marketing food was largely a problem of adequate transport facilities which required much labour to provide. Secondly, with the change in social standards mass migration demands special measures to be taken at the receiving end. Some publicists have proposed that "new

[1] *Ibid.*, pp. 54–55.

towns" should be built in Australia, for example; 20,000 immigrants at a time could be housed and employed, but neither the economic organization nor the economic surplus exists to provide for immigrants on such a lavish scale in that country.[1]   Housing is a serious problem for Australians as for others; and the policy of "houses first, immigrants later" is unrealistic if advocated simultaneously with a plan for greatly increased mass immigration.

Asiatic migrations on a huge scale are open to similar objections.   They are, in addition, susceptible to two other weaknesses.   First, most possible Asiatic or African "reception areas" are themselves well populated in relation to their economic resources, and the level of their productive techniques.   Mass immigration would mean great capital outlays per head of immigrants.   Secondly, in these economically and socially "backward" areas emigration would have little or no effect on the population problem, or the economic problem, of the country from which the emigrants come. (Selective emigration is another matter altogether, as it may have educational and cultural advantages that can be turned to economic benefit, e.g., if Indians settle in the U.S. and provide an educational training centre for Indian students there.)

While the ratio of land to the other factors may have been brought into less striking disharmony in some instances, there still remain very substantial differences, not so much perhaps between land and labour as between capital of an appropriate kind and labour.   Theoretically, therefore, economic gain may accrue from a movement of workers in a direction which tends to equalize more nearly

[1] See Barker, 1948, for a statement of this case, and Plant, 1951, for the counter-arguments.   A plan for mass emigration to African territories was put forward by Leone in 1951.

the capital per head of the countries between which the flow takes place, or, more accurately, to optimize the ratio between capital goods (some of them specific) and population.

Economic gain *may* accrue from a movement of persons to countries where output per head is relatively high, and the evidence (for instance, the mere fact of the more or less successful large-scale emigration of the post-war years) seems to confirm that in certain instances it *does* accrue.

There are, moreover, some powerful political (in which are here included social) obstacles to movement. The country of origin is losing its citizens who may be leaving to acquire a new social outlook and way of life. Its cultural survival is threatened.

The economic loss to the country of origin may not be negligible, since it has incurred the whole cost of educating and rearing the young person who now proceeds to spend his or her active life elsewhere. This loss has become far more serious in modern times than ever before, because of the extension of the period of upbringing and education, and because of the increasing expenses of medical care and social benefits. In the same way, other expenses arising for social security make emigration economically unattractive to countries of origin. They are liable to be left with an unduly high proportion of old age pensioners, permanently sick people, and children to support, with a low proportion of active persons on whom taxes to meet these various expenses can be imposed. Some advocates of mass migration have, indeed, discussed the possibility of charges such as these being shared in some way between "losing" and "gaining" countries.[1]

Plans for mass migration may be regarded as unproved

[1] See Sauvy, 1948.

remedies for the economically maldistributed population of the world, as a general rule, although no doubt from time to time mass movements will be advocated. Apart from economic arguments there are several political arguments used in their favour: first, the arguments in favour of the dispersion of such specially placed populations as that of Great Britain[1]; secondly, the need to secure homogeneous populations and to avoid continual strife has prompted such new countries as Pakistan and India to encourage mass exchanges of population; and thirdly, the policy of allowing asylum to the ideologically dissatisfied, or to the genuinely oppressed, has led to the large refugee problem, which up to 1953 has flowed in Europe from east to west on balance, with a trickle the other way.

These political mass migrations, whether contemplated or already taking place, cause rather than spring from economic problems. They will affect in a fairly unpredictable way the population trends of the countries where they occur. It seems safe to say, however, that a mass dispersal (of, say, 20–30 millions in a decade) of Western European citizens to destinations overseas will not take place, for the same objections raised to such mass migrations, when advocated on economic grounds, apply to this proposal equally effectively. The initial economic costs of such movements are prohibitive. But very large mass movements of the scale of 3–4 millions in five years are still economically feasible.[2]

The political factors affecting migration are not so wholly unpredictable as might be supposed, for they are

[1] Here, the mass migration of 20 of Britain's 50 millions is a figure that has been much discussed in recent years.

[2] There are likely to be cyclical fluctuations in the movements, so it is not safe to assume that ten times these numbers will be likely to move in fifty years.

closely linked to economic trends. It has been seen that each of the two power blocks of the world includes large and rapidly growing populations among its power-assets, but there is one important difference. The two largest Communist powers have a geographically internal "frontier" territory to develop, the Russians in their eastern and south-eastern possessions, the Chinese in their north and west. If the stagnationists are, after all, right, this existence of a virtual "frontier" gives a considerable stimulus to the economic growth of the Russian and Chinese economies.

The two largest Communist powers have themselves no shortage of population in an absolute sense, and within the Russian orbit are satellites with a fairly high rate of increase. Thus, even if Russia has some temporary man-power problems, these can be solved without recourse to manpower from, say, Italy or Germany. With the advantages of both an extensive frontier to develop and adequate numbers for growth, the Communist powers can look forward to a natural increase in their strength.

The Americans' position must not be over-contrasted with that of their rivals. Every country has, as it were, an intensive as well as an extensive frontier, and the Americans have hitherto been especially skilful at their development of an internal market, and at intensive capital formation. But their extensive frontiers lie out-side their own territory. The new lands which they can most naturally develop on an extensive basis are in Canada, South America and Africa. This means that the United States must either conquer, dominate, or co-operate with a number of its allies.

So far as political "trends" are concerned, the flow of migration must be towards the frontier territories wherever they are found, and towards the cities and towns. No other main kinds of flow would be compatible with the maintenance or growth of political power.

If, then, the 1953 division of the world into power blocks continues, sooner or later the "Western" leaders may want to re-open the question of German, Italian and Japanese settlement overseas, for these are the nationalities whose rural populations are numerous enough to provide a surplus suitable for transfer. At the same time other countries of the non-Soviet or Chinese bloc category will want to see that migration takes place on a sufficient scale to relieve population pressure, or to maintain political links.

But the economic changes which are contemplated in various parts of the world may create a migration problem far more acute than any political upheaval has done to date.

There are three reasons why economic development may be hostile to large populations in backward countries. First, these countries are moving from "feudalism", or some system of local oppression, to more advanced forms of economic organization. This kind of move is liable to provoke an acute short-term shortage of food and necessities, for reasons that were touched on in the discussion of "optimum" populations. The old oppressive class may perforce have to withdraw its support from the "tertiary" employees whom it kept occupied, and the new, perhaps more egalitarian, regime will not spend the surplus which it has appropriated in such a way as to offer substitute employment. Or the old oppressive class will "reform" itself, and adopt new methods of agriculture, as England did during the enclosure movement, or as the landlords did in Ireland during the period of the evictions. These sudden improvements in agricultural technique may throw millions of people off the land;

this might happen in a country like Egypt if, for some reason, a much less labour-heavy technique of cultivation suddenly became profitable.   Secondly, economic development may cause straightforward technological unemployment if, for instance, machines are introduced which wipe out the demand for labour, total demand not rising fast enough to maintain employment.   Finally, the growth of both manufactures and agriculture, though rapid in the developing countries, may not be rapid enough to avoid "frictional" setbacks, which may in some instances imply huge temporary unemployment or even famine.   In the short run economic development of a "backward" country may bring disaster.

It is to be hoped that this possibility is widely enough feared to make avoidance of it reasonably probable.   But the sudden collapse of a single export industry, or the too sudden adoption of some new techniques of agriculture, would provoke in any one backward country an immense pressure to emigrate.   An acute problem of finding a suitable reception area would then face the United Nations.

Thus, although there has been a downward trend in the relative importance of migration since the nineteenth century, the conclusion must be drawn that this trend may be reversed.   With economic development new streams of emigrants may appear.

§ 3. *Short-term International Migration.*   So far the discussion has been confined to long-term or "permanent" international migration, that is to the movement of "settlers" from country to country.   Many people, however, cross frontiers without the intention of living the rest of their lives outside their country of origin.   They are of four classes: seafarers or railwaymen, tourists, seasonal workers, and semi-permanent migrants usually to particular industries abroad; some of all these, particularly of the last two categories, may become permanent migrants, just as, conversely, some of the would-be permanent migrants eventually return home.[1]

Seafarers and tourists can be omitted from any lengthy consideration, although even these categories play some part in the prospecting of new ways of living, and in the growth of cities and towns. Seaports all over the world attract settlers of different nationalities; seas, it is said, like rivers, naturally unite and do not divide, the divisions often being political or social in origin, rather than economic or individual.

It is incorrect to think of world population as entirely static, of people as being rooted to their homes until a sudden change occurs. They are perpetually oscillating, like the electrons in a gas, darting here or there, mostly of course on short journeys, but to a considerable extent across frontiers, until for some reason or other the pull becomes strong enough to fix them in a new habitat; and the individual then, perhaps, pursues a new and shorter daily oscillatory path (to and from his work, to holiday places and so on). There can be little doubt that the consequence of seasonal and semi-permanent migration is that permanent migration becomes more practicable. For the seasonal worker, like the agricultural workers moving into France from Spain at harvest time, may make friends and establish social contacts that eventually lead him to live in a French village; or the male workers brought into the mines from Poland or Italy may decide to stay in England or France, or wherever the mines are,

[1] According to a calculation of Willcox 35–39 per cent of migrants entering the U.S. in the twenty-three years to 1914 returned home within the same period; the backflow was 15 per cent from 1923–30, and over 100 per cent during the Depression.

and to send for their families.   Short-term migration is a useful method of solving some of the economic problems of the geographical uneven distribution of labour without grave commitments being entered upon.

Unfortunately it is nearly always the receiving country that secures these benefits, the idea often being that if there is any unemployment the immigrants are to be the first to be thrown out of work, and if necessary deported. From an international point of view this is a reprehensible practice, but it does not directly concern us as a population matter.

The main point about the seasonal and semi-permanent migration of workers is that it satisfies in practice the need which theory foresaw for some safety-valve.   Short of complete migration, which is hampered by various important economic and social frictions, there are these intermediate stages in the movement of population. These short-term movements deserve, therefore, very careful study, since they are pointers to the relative economic and demographic structures of the economies between which they take place on any scale.

§ 4. *Migration and Trade Cycles.*   For many years economists have speculated upon the relation between migration and fluctuations in general economic activity.   In relation to population change, migration is mainly important for its long-term effects.   Short-term fluctuations are significant only so far as they affect the trend.

Whether there are very long cycles in economic affairs still remains an undecided question.   Kondratieff concluded, in his well-known article of 1926,[1] from the

[1] Of which a translation appeared in the *Review of Economic Statistics*, Vol. XVII, No. 6, November 1935, p. 105, which was reprinted in *Readings in Business Cycle Theory*, 1950, p. 20.

statistical evidence then available, that "the existence of long waves of cyclical character is very probable." The course of economic development proceeded, he thought, through a series of long as well as of short waves. His first "wave" lasted for about sixty years from 1780, the second for forty-seven years, and the third had not concluded at the time that his contribution was made.

If there are long cycles, lasting half-centuries—or perhaps others persisting for a hundred or two hundred years —can they be identified and measured, and can useful predictions be based upon them? Professor Hicks, in the famous footnote with which he concluded his well-known theoretical work,[1] threw out the startling suggestion that the industrial revolution lasting two hundred years was perhaps a very long secular boom, and that, if so, it might have been largely due to the unparalleled increase in population. He somewhat cryptically remarked that this would help to explain why, "as the wisest hold, it has been such a disappointing episode in human history". But why should a boom lasting for two hundred years be such a disappointing event? In itself, such a result would seem to be a matter for rejoicing. Professor Hicks's point must be not that the boom as such was bad, but that because it was *only* a boom it was bound to come to an end—how and when it would end, the context shows, Professor Hicks was too cautious to forecast, since this would depend on the virtually unpredictable trend of innovations in techniques.

The central issue of the problem of the long-term cycle, if there is one, is indeed this issue of what direction the trend of innovation is likely to follow, and what character the innovations are to have. For most economists would agree (with varying degrees of emphasis) that great stress

[1] Hicks, 1946, p. 302.

must be laid on the supply of investment opportunities which is provided by invention and innovation; therefore they would accept the view that it is important that there should be a sufficient amount of innovation to keep the factors of production more or less fully employed.

There would be less agreement on the importance of the character of the innovations. The subject has been in dispute ever since Ricardo re-wrote his chapter on machinery. The extreme *laissez-faire* view would be that in the very long run the character of the innovations was of no importance. What matters, on this view, is that the cheapest method of production should always be followed. In the long run this will result in output per head, and hence real income, being as great as it is possible for it to be. In the short run, of course, the innovation may be extremely labour-saving, and so cause unemployment and starvation among displaced workers, but, on this view, such short-term evils need short-term remedies.

The more historically-minded schools of economists attach some importance to the character of the innovations. They think that it may matter very much, even in the long run, whether an innovation is labour-saving or labour-complementary. The technological unemployment caused by the first type of innovation may have, they argue, long-run repercussions; and if this is not accepted, they fall back on Keynes's aphorism on long runs.

The relevance of this debate to the present problem is that migration is, economically, the adjustment in space of the low-paid worker to the (relatively) high-paid job opportunity. The adjustment does not take place easily, and there are many frictions to slow down or divert movement, but as a long-run phenomenon migration should roughly tend to correspond to that ideal adjustment that the *laissez-faire* theorist depicts. Or, alternatively, it should flow in the directions which, on a historical view, are most likely to be beneficial, having regard to stability of employment and to such other additional criteria as the historicist wishes to introduce.

For the interpretation of the mass migrations of the last two hundred years the *laissez-faire* theory is perhaps useful to this extent: that it emphasizes the increase in output per head resulting from the movements that took place. On the other hand, the social and economic frictions to movement must not be overlooked; just as, even under free trade, purchasing power parity of different currencies is rarely complete, so real output per head, and real wages, vary from country to country, not only in the short but in the long run. The migration of workers which could bring them into equality fails to take place because of cost of movement, the inertia of existing arrangements, and social factors, such as the desire for propinquity to friends, and for the sharing of a common language.

What tends to be left out of either extreme economic or extreme historical determinism is the importance of acts of choice, when strategic decisions are taken. This process goes on continuously. There are strategic decisions taken by investors, and those who decide what types of capital equipment are to be made; and other strategic decisions are taken by consumers, not only the "seigneurs" of Professor Sauvy's illustrative examples but by consumers as a whole, whenever they have a surplus to spend above that necessary to purchase conventional necessities. If Mr. Jones decides, permanently, to give up smoking and to visit the theatre weekly, the total, as well as the partial, demand for labour is thereby affected. The importance of this type of decision is hardly likely to be recognized when it is relegated to the dull category labelled "change of taste".

In the nineteenth century these matters were very fully debated, and strategic decisions were taken to develop a type of civilization which was particularly well suited *both* to a very rapid increase in population *and* to a high long-term rate of migration. The detailed history of these decisions cannot be set out here, but the broad points can be fairly clearly recognized. First, there was the decision to "improve agriculture", which involved enclosure Acts. The social consequences of this were seen first in England, and later, even more acutely, in Ireland; in the mid-nineteenth century the agrarian revolution affected Germany as well. Many people had to leave the land as the decades went by (some precipitately, when a harvest failed). Secondly, there were the innovations in transport, which involved a steady high demand for labour, and also meant that much larger urban concentrations were now becoming economically possible. Thirdly, there were the legislative changes, which abolished paternalistic regulation of economic affairs (the Speenhamland system, and the control of prices and usury), so exposing the increasing masses of people deliberately to economic pressure. Fourthly, it was decided, on balance, that the manufacturing interests of a nation were paramount, since the greatest increases in real wealth seemed to lie chiefly in their capacity; the textile, iron and steel, and coal industries received an especial fillip, and both old and new markets for their products were captured or developed. Fifthly, with the new surpluses of real incomes accruing (over and above minimum needs) to certain social groups "tertiary" occupations of many kinds became economically more attractive. Clerking, advertising, domestic service and holiday resorts flourished.

All five of these points are characteristics of nineteenth-century England, which increased apparently its real wage-rates per head, as did Germany, Belgium and other countries, with extraordinary rapidity between 1860 and 1890, although in the period from 1890 to 1913 a kind of plateau was reached, due to what Professor Phelps-Brown has labelled a "climacteric".[1] This check to progress was not, according to some distinguished contemporary observers, inevitable. It resulted perhaps from a strategic decision by managers and trade unionists to take life more easily, to buy leisure and relaxation rather than progress with their efforts. But another important reason, both for the rapidity of the nineteenth-century advance and for the slowing down of the 1890's, was the stage then reached by technological development. As Professor Phelps-Brown has pointed out, the really large-scale *application* of the inventions associated with steam and steel had been made by the 1890's; thereafter the vast processes of re-equipping must have been complete, and all that remained to do was replacement. The *new* techniques coming along, in electricity, internal combustion engines and chemicals, did not reach the stage of large-scale application for some decades.

Rapid and unprecedented as the mid-nineteenth-century advance was in Great Britain, it did not suffice to give full employment to the population that was still growing, as natural increase remained high. The great developments partly depended upon, as well as inspired, an increase in population, indeed, a very large increase in population; but they were not sufficient to keep the whole British and Irish population within these islands. For exactly the same reasons as they were wanted at home, people were also wanted abroad. The age of steam and

1 Phelps-Brown with Handfield-Jones, 1952.

steel came to the United States only a little later than to this country; corresponding developments also began in what is now the Commonwealth.

Migration of a long-term kind has not necessarily come to an end. But it will not cease merely because there are now no longer any geographically undiscovered corners of the earth worth talking about. In the first place, many parts of the earth *are* still unprospected, in the economic sense. New techniques are available for prospecting them much more rapidly than in the past. The search for raw materials may create new townships and cities, in quite remote and even unexpected places. Secondly, the massive application of new techniques may yet require labour in large quantities. Thirdly, even with our knowledge limited to existing techniques, any density map of the world suggests that there must yet remain strong economic tendencies for a substantial movement of peoples.

On a long-term view fairly large-scale international migration appears, indeed, to be unavoidable. Just how it is to take place, and how the worst frictions that it implies are to be avoided, is a problem that will occupy several generations of statesmen.

Migration has fluctuated with trade cycles since 1913, although, according to the data analysed by Professor Brinley Thomas,[1] the tendency before that date was for the building cycle, which is believed to be longer than the usual trade cycle, to have the greater effect. Consequently, in the earlier period, when Britain was having a constructional slump the U.S. was having a constructional boom, and emigration actually tended to be relatively high.

Professor Thomas, like Professor Brown, detects an

[1] Thomas, 1951, p. 215.

14

important structural change in the British, indeed in the Atlantic, economy occurring in the 1890's.[1] This, he believes, accounts for the failure of British economic development in the period 1897–1913 to fit into the Kondratieff pattern—a failure discussed at length by Schumpeter.

Short-term fluctuations in migration are presumably inevitable so long as short-term cycles occur, whether they are "building cycles" or "trade cycles", or simply cycles generated by speculation or recurrent political crises. A severe recent fluctuation has occurred in Australian immigration policy. Migration, being in a sense marginal to an economy, is always liable to suffer more than any other kind of human activity. (One of the distressing features of short-term migration has been the tendency of the receiving country to regard immigrants as a cushion, to be used, by deportation, in case of a slump.)

If men were all "economic men", in a rather strictly abstract sense, desiring only the fruits of "output per head" in general and not particular satisfactions, most countries would allow and encourage far more immigration than in fact they do. For the cost of rearing a child, and educating him or her, is heavy, and economic gain would accrue to a country which took full advantage of any surpluses of labour overseas, and cut down its birth-rate to a minimum. A mature, civilized state is, indeed, somewhat liable to pursue this policy, especially when its civilization is highly cerebral, and it places high economic value upon education and not much upon the pleasures of domesticity. Thus it pursues, by choice, a policy which would inevitably be pursued by a state in which all men coldly aimed at an "economic maximum". The

[1] *Ibid.*, p. 250. Like Professor Brown he associates the change with the era of electricity, internal combustion and chemicals.

final logical step to take is to import slaves, or persons with no civic rights, or a minimum of rights, so that labour supply is bought like a commodity. Why should any adults have children of their own, from an economic point of view? In agrarian societies there are clear reasons, or in societies where people have reason to fear their old age if they have no issue; but in modern industrial societies, with some social security and no possibility of economic reward from children the motives disappear.

These propositions offer a *reductio ad absurdum* to the argument that population matters, and especially questions affecting migration, can be considered as economic questions, in total isolation from assumptions about "ends", or from assumptions about "tastes"—such as the "taste" for having a family of one's own.

There are fairly strong economic arguments in favour not only of large-scale migration on a permanent basis, but for greater freedom of short-term movements. Studies in the United States have shown how important a part large-scale internal migration plays in that country—on a continental scale. The economic benefits of such movements, if they could be free elsewhere, are probably very great. But the social and political objections to a greatly increased flow of persons, though sometimes ill-founded, cannot all be brushed aside; many of them could be overcome if international agencies handling the detailed arrangements were well staffed, and provided with adequate funds. Civilization may be enriched, not threatened, by migration, so long as the flow does not lead to worsened or new forms of racial or nationalistic rivalry.

PART III

FUTURE PROSPECTS

CHAPTER IX

GREAT BRITAIN

How many people there will be in Great Britain fifty years hence can be estimated only if some complex of demographic, economic and political events can be predicted; modern population theory affords no safe basis of prediction, unlike a theory which ascribes to human reproductiveness an unchanging value. Moreover, no modern theory can fail to take some account of both internal and international migration.

How many people there ought to be in Britain at that date is an even more widely debatable question, answerable according to the values and objectives that are held to be paramount. Clear simple answers to our problems must almost necessarily be unsound, so great and numerous are our present uncertainties.

Fortunately, however, this does not mean that Britain's population problem cannot be rationally debated. Results in some ranges are more likely than results outside those ranges, and some sizes of population are likely, in the event, to be "better", by acceptable criteria, than others.

§ 1. *Demographic, Economic, Political and Social Objectives and Factors.* To avoid repetition, this chapter will be divided into two, rather than three, main sections; in the first section demographic and economic considerations will be reviewed together, and in the second there will be a brief discussion of political and social factors.

The thesis advanced here is that the economic factors

outweigh the others.   For there are facts from which it can be argued that the key factors, in the case of Britain, determining its population size, are likely to be economic more preponderantly than demographic or political, important though these two classes of influence may also be.   In this respect Britain, in the mid-twentieth century, is not necessarily typical; other countries at the same date, or Britain at different dates, may have been influenced less by economic than by demographic or social forces and developments.   Britain by the mid-twentieth century was at a point in its historical development when its demographic structure was comparatively stable and controlled.   Its political future, though uncertain, seemed fairly likely to lie within a range of possibilities none of which would affect the population that it could support quite so seriously as would its economic strength, although of course some unforeseen political cataclysm could easily upset this balance of different forces.

Past trends have been used by some writers to show first, that Britain's population *will* be, and secondly that it *ought* to be, either smaller than, or equal to, its 1950 size.

Britain's demographic position is not strong, however, in that it has an aging population and a rather sharply falling number of persons in the more fecund age-groups. Its population pyramid does not suggest expansion in the near future, unless family size habits were to be suddenly and substantially changed, and it suggests that even to maintain the present size of population by natural increase will require a change in the broad downward trend in the habit of reproducing children.   For reasons of this kind those who argue on the basis of demographic projections alone generally estimate that the British population will in 1975 be of about the same size as it was in 1950,[1] and rather less (though perhaps not much less) by the year 2000. Demographically speaking, a continued population of 50 millions in Britain for another half-century is to be regarded as a fairly high achievement, and a somewhat lower figure is usually thought to be more probable.

There is no doubt that demographic factors are of great importance. If there are no fertile wives of sufficient strength or will-power to bear children (or an insufficiency of these with a given pattern of family size), or if there is an insufficiency of virile husbands, clearly the population must in the long run decline accordingly. Demography, in this somewhat platitudinous sense, is the paramount factor. Even so, other factors may still have their effects (for instance, if the fecundity and strength of the mothers is a function of the food supply, and this in turn a function of economic organization). But in the second half of the twentieth century Britain's population is not, even in this limited sense, likely to be mainly determined by demographic forces. The demographic forces are themselves much more likely to be both outweighed, and operated upon, by economic conditions, and the range of demographic possibilities is too wide for these forces alone to be at all a safe basis for prediction.

Statistics are, by their very nature, incapable of "proving" this point, but they run in a way not inconsistent with its likelihood. For example, there can be little doubt that, to the extent that other things are equal, the birth-rate has risen in the twentieth century in

[1] See, for example, not only the Royal Commission's projections (already quoted above) but also the estimates of the Materials Policy Commission, 1952, Vol. II, p. 131. M. Bourgeois-Pichat estimated a 2 per cent growth in the population of England and Wales between 1950 and 1980 (quoted in the *Economic Survey of Europe Since the War*, 1953, p. 160), his estimate being based on prospective natural increase alone, exclusive of migration.

Britain with prosperous economic conditions, and fallen in less prosperous conditions. The *extent* of this rise and fall cannot be definitively measured because of the effects of long-term trends, which certainly exist but cannot be eliminated except by an ultimately arbitrary estimate, and the changing internal structure of the population in respect of occupation, place of residence, social status and other vital non-"demographic" factors, which again can be only imperfectly measured. But the fact of the rise and fall is well established, and makes some apparent "demographic" movements more correctly describable as g in our notation, that is cyclical economic effects.

When economic conditions fluctuated slowly and in long waves the longer- and medium-term demographic factors (a and b) may well have been better worth selecting as of paramount importance. But in the twentieth century two world wars and one world slump have affected Britain (excluding Ireland of course) far more profoundly in a few years than any single economic or political event of the nineteenth century ever did. The short- and medium-term political and economic factors have become paramount.

Left to themselves the long-term demographic factors seem to imply a diminishing population in Britain within the half-century, or at most a very slight growth. But the history of the first half of the twentieth century suggests that these factors will not remain undisturbed; demography is like the spring of a mantelshelf clock, the strength of which is known. But we do not know whether the master of the house (or some interfering guest) may not rewind the clock, alter its speed, or even manipulate the hands. We cannot therefore predict, on the basis of the spring alone, what time its dial will record at a given interval from 1950; we have to arrive at some guess how serious the outside disturbances will be.

There are, however, reasons for supposing that the demographic structure of the country is less unstable than at some earlier periods, and also better controlled. By "stable" is here meant resistant to herd-like changes in mass behaviour, or to the effects of other great changes, which implies that greater "control", or choice, is exercised by individual parents in their decisions on the sizes of their families. In the nineteenth century a fall in the death-rate almost inevitably meant a large rise in population, the main reason for this being that the rate at which potential parents had children was liable to continue at its previous high level. A similar situation prevails in many backward countries to-day. But in Britain a fall in the death-rate would not provide a similarly firm basis for predicting a rapid increase in population, not merely because specific death-rates are already low for the child-bearing age-groups of women, but also because of the rapidity with which an educated and culturally advanced community can adjust its births to its mortality situation. Whether, in any particular circumstance, the power of control *will* be exercised is a particular question; that it *can* be exercised (it sometimes has been) in Britain is now beyond dispute.

§ 2. *Economic Arguments for a Stable or Falling Population.*
Many powerful economic arguments can be brought to support the demographers' view that Britain's population will never much exceed 50 millions, and that it will probably fall (and certainly *ought* to fall) below that figure. These economic arguments for a smaller population are fourfold, relating to land, labour, capital and overseas trade.

First, with regard to land, that term has several different economic meanings. In its simplest possible sense it denotes a sector of the earth's surface. So far, but only so far, as agriculture is extensive this is a relevant sense. The density of population to land in the United Kingdom is 0·342 per hectare (or of land to population 2·92 hectares per head); for England and Wales alone the figure is 0·477 per hectare (that is only 2·1 hectares per head).[1] If countries are ranked by density, England and Wales come out rather high in the list.[2] The figures tend to sound more frightening when expressed as "persons per square mile"; 2·1 hectares per head (i.e., about 5 acres) does not sound so bad, until it is recalled that the figure includes *all* land, and not only land used for, or available for, agriculture.

The density figure in itself proves neither that population is too dense, nor that the country could economically become even more thickly populated. Economists who fear a shortage of Britain's land in this connection are (or should be) thinking less of the overall density figure than of the amount of cultivable land available, and of the cost of maintaining it cultivated. Land, as a unit of extension, is the subject of many competing demands. The naturally best land agriculturally for miles around often tends to be near the towns; indeed its existence there may have been one reason for the siting, and growth, of the town in that position. The competing demands of the town for land may thus not only take land away from agriculture but some of the naturally "best", and more or less irreplace-

[1] For England alone, without Wales, 0·522 or 1·9 hectares a head. This can be converted into acres per head by multiplying by 2½.

[2] In population per square kilometre England and Wales had a figure of 291, just below the Netherlands, 312, and above Belgium, 283, but well below the 500 of the Egyptian Nile Valley or the 360 of some Indonesian islands (see *Preliminary Report on the World Social Situation*, U.N. Dept. of Social Affairs, New York, 1952).

able-land.   Well-known examples are the land of the Lea Valley near London, and the market-garden land to the west of Hammersmith, and the fertile strip that lies between Birmingham and Coventry.

Cultivable land in Britain is limited, and is evidently scarcer than in many other countries.   This will not be a factor of importance in restricting the growth of British population *unless* this land has to be used at a cost so extravagantly uneconomic (that is, so dear) that population would be better served by emigration on a mass scale, or that families can no longer be supported at a tolerable standard of living, or that actual starvation must set in.   Those who regard the limited quantity of land as a major factor, now, and in the near future, limiting population growth, fear one or other of these dangers.

It will be argued below that these fears, in respect of British agriculture, though by no means groundless, are less overwhelming than they may appear at first sight. There are reasons for supposing that the dangers envisaged may be staved off in the future as in the past, although not necessarily by following the same policies as heretofore.

§ 3. *The Supply of Raw Materials.*   Many raw materials were "plentiful" per head of population in the early days of Britain's industrial revolution : iron ore and lead, as well as coal, copper and tin, were exported in the first half of the nineteenth century, whereas now Britain is deficient, in relation to its own and to the world's demands, of every raw material except coal, which itself is surplus to domestic demand only in exceptional years—and will be deficient permanently from about 1960, according to current estimates.   There are far fewer counter-arguments available than to the allegation that Britain's agricultural

potential is too low.   The raw material position is undoubtedly very serious.   Britain cannot live as an industrial nation without an assured flow of imports of raw
materials.   Those who forecast an interruption to that
flow, for whatever reason, rightly draw attention to the
corollary that Britain's population, in those circumstances,
would be too great.

If a cross-classification is made, those raw materials
which are the sources of power may be regarded as having
special importance for an industrial country.   Until very
recently the main fuel materials were coal, oil, natural
gas and water-power.   Coal and lignite provided [1] 47 per
cent of the world's energy supplies, and liquid fuels 20 per
cent, the rest being supplied by natural gas (7 per cent)
and hydro-electricity (6 per cent), or being provided in
unrecorded ways by non-commercial sources (19 per
cent).   In units of "coal equivalent" the use in mid-
century varied from less than half a ton per head per
annum used in Asia, to over 7 tons a head used in North
America.   If the countries using over $1\frac{1}{2}$ tons a head are
classed as "developed", this will include North America,
Northern Europe, Oceania, the Union of South Africa
and the U.S.S.R., and exclude the rest of the world.
Europe and North America produced and consumed
72 per cent of the world's solid fuels in 1949.   The "developed areas" as a whole produced and consumed some
88 per cent, and also provided 30 million tons of coal for
under-developed countries or ships' bunkers.   Europe as
a whole was much more dependent for its energy upon
solid fuels, however, than was North America.

The position with regard to liquid fuel sources was very

[1] Based on figures for 1949 (U.N. Statistical Papers, Series J, No. 1,
World Energy Supplies in Selected Years, 1929–1950, New York,
September 1952).

different.   Europe produced less than 2 per cent of the world's crude oil, but consumed 11 per cent of the world total.

Europe's share of world production of solid fuels declined between 1929 and 1950 (from 48 per cent to 41 per cent), and Britain's share declined even more steeply than this.[1]   This trend seems likely to continue, as new sources of solid fuel are opened up in less developed parts of the world.

In 1929 Britain's consumption of commercial fuel per head (in tons of "coal equivalent") was greater than that of any other European country except Belgium, at 4·11 tons against Belgium's 4·53; by 1950 Britain's average had risen to 4·42 against Belgium's 3·50.   Norway and Sweden also had high figures of use of energy resources.

Britain's fuel position over the next fifty years can hardly be discussed seriously except in relation to that of Western Europe as a whole, and to the world political situation.   For evidently any substantial rise in its fuel usage per head to, say, the level reached by the U.S. in 1937 (5·89 tons a head), or 1950 (7·51 tons a head), would imply a linking of Britain's electricity industry with continental hydro-electric sources, or heavy coal imports, or much heavier liquid fuel imports from a peaceful Middle East.   It is also, of course, vital that Britain should succeed in expanding its own coal output, but the most optimistic planners could hardly suppose that all the energy needed could be derived from this source of fuel.   It seems, indeed, more likely that for economic as well as technological reasons British coal will become in an increasing proportion a raw material, and that other sources of energy will be sought and developed, such as atomic power.

---

[1] From 19 to 14 per cent.

Evidently Britain's industrial growth, and therefore the population that it can support, depends upon, among other factors, the solution it finds to the problem of fuel Atomic energy may have become commercial by the end of the period.

The point for population growth is, however, this: whatever solution is found in detail it will demand, so far as can now be seen, a very heavy capital investment. If *no* solution is found, then the economy must tend to contract, and so must the population; if *any* solution is found, in any of the directions that now seem even remotely feasible, an investment must be incurred so great as to demand at least as large a working population as the present, and possibly a larger one, in order to gain economic results from a huge indivisible expenditure.

Those who argue that fuel supplies will dictate a smaller population must rest their case, therefore, on the belief that the fuel problem will be only partially solved, and that, if increased energy per head is required, it will be obtained not by tapping new sources of energy, but by reducing the number of "heads ' and making full use of the limited resources available within our boundaries, or purchasable at a reasonable price on the world markets.

§ 4. *The Balance of Payments Argument.*   Britain's balance of payments problems are short-term, medium-term and long-term.   The effective case against a growing population in Britain over the next fifty years must rest on a long-term analysis.

Three propositions are usually advanced.   The first is that, however much world production expands over the next fifty years, world trade is unlikely to expand so much, and may hardly expand at all.   The second is that Britain will be competing, in this narrow world market for exports, with a few powerful rivals, as well as with smaller but rising competitors, and that both these classes will be strategically well placed to secure together an increasing share of the limited world trade at Britain's expense (the best to be hoped for Britain being a stationary share). Finally, the third proposition is that the volume of imports required by Britain will be geared to the size of its population. Each of these propositions is defensible in the light of past experience, and together they add up to a formidable argument in favour of a static or reduced British population.

The first proposition depends on the extrapolation of a trend that was very marked between 1913 and 1939. Between those dates, world manufacturing production approximately doubled, but the volume of world trade in manufactures failed to rise.[1] Some observers [2] think that the long-term downward trend of foreign trade in manufactures as a proportion of industrial output must persist, at least until 1960; but few have prognosticated a reversal of the trend at a later date. If so, by 1960 world trade in manufactures may not be more than 40–50 per cent above the 1937 level. Britain's share of this trade rose to 23 per cent in 1950, as against 19 per cent in 1937, but thereafter fell, concomitantly with the industrial re-emergence of Germany and Japan on world markets. On Professor Robinson's calculations of Britain's chances to earn currencies by exports (visible and invisible), not more than 80 per cent of the volume of 1938 imports can readily be financed in 1960. He suggests that the moral is that the economic system will have to be adjusted to be viable with a long-term lower level of imports. Some would

[1] MacDougall, 1947, p. 85, and see *Industrialization and Foreign Trade* (League of Nations, 1945), p. 157, and Diagram VII, p. 226, where an index for mining and manufacturing is shown.
[2] E.g., Robinson, A., 1953, p. 3.

evidently proceed from his argument to the corollary that
British population is too great.

The second proposition is based on the judgment that
Britain's foreign competitors are going to be strategically
better placed to develop foreign sales than Britain will
be.   In 1952 about 75 per cent of world exports in manufactures was in the hands of seven leading countries—the
U.S.A., the U.K., West Germany, France, Canada,
Belgium and Switzerland.   An eighth country, Japan,
seemed likely soon to rise to about the fifth place.   The
U.S.A. and the U.K. had by far the largest individual
shares.[1]   It has been shown that even in 1950 the U.K.'s
share of trade in general had declined as compared with
1937, and in 1937 there had already been a heavy fall in
the percentage of world trade accruing to the U.K. and
to France, while the shares of the U.S.A., Japan and
Canada had risen very substantially, and those of Sweden,
Belgium and Germany quite noticeably, since 1913.   Thus
Britain has a twofold problem: of selling against the keen
rivalry of a few of the most industrialized countries in
the world, which have, moreover, several sources of
economic strength as exporters that are not available to
Britain, and secondly, of meeting the competition of less
powerful but rising industrial nations springing up all
over the world.

The first part of this problem is, in effect, that Britain
is in an especially vulnerable position in relation to the
wider world issues of chronic dollar shortage and industrialization of under-developed areas.   The second part
is due to the compound interest effect of any economic
advantage, one kind of relative economic strength paving
the way to a more than proportionate acquisition of
another.

[1] *Ibid.*, 1953, p. 3.

Britain's trade relations with Brazil in recent years, for example, aptly illustrate both these difficulties. At a time when Brazil was flourishing in boom conditions and attracting more and more American capital, and with that capital developing a two-way trade with the U.S., Britain had to curtail its trade with Brazil owing to bad debts and currency difficulties; it would seem that the economic power of the U.S. suffices to override bad debts and Brazil's own dollar shortage, both of which are nearly fatal to the development of a healthy non-dollar trade. Britain would not be able to play a large part in the industrialization of under-developed areas, nor to compete effectively in the world market for industrial products, if its financial liquidity remained low.

The third proposition is based upon a judgment as to the future of British agriculture, on the character of Britain's social and economic development, and on the likely future terms of trade for agricultural products, raw materials and other imports deemed necessary to this country.

§ 5. *Counter-Arguments (Demographic and Economic) in Favour of a Stable or Increasing Population.* Arguments on demography, where they proceed from factual statements to normative assertions, unavoidably are based upon social views or social prejudices. Demography as a science provides techniques of analysis, not results or conclusions. In the particular case of Great Britain there are no demographic facts that suffice to support the view that the British population *must* fall, or *must* stay stable, over the next fifty years. Family size has declined, but not in such a way, or for so long a period, as makes it impossible to imagine that population might not again rise by natural increase.

The birth-rate of Great Britain is the result, so it is contended here, mainly of the social and economic environmental conditions, rather than of some underlying trend in family-building behaviour, determined by internal or external forces of a non-economic character. That British populations are still capable of high rates of natural increase is sufficiently proved by the birth-rates that prevail among the European settlers of Northern Rhodesia, for example, and by the high proportion at home of unmarried females aged 18 to 24.

What are the main economic factors that are likely to affect the possibility, and desirability, of Britain supporting a larger population over the next fifty years? Those at present known to be likely are the opening up of new sources of raw materials, the development of new forms of power, the increasing application of scientific knowledge to the supply of food (both in agricultural techniques and in the development of synthetic processes), the bringing of the simpler kinds of capital equipment into co-operation with the reserves of underemployed labour of the world, the mass application of scientific and technical development to ways of building, distribution and domestic work, and a widening of the capital already invested into means of large-scale transport. All these processes have begun; it is not idle speculation to assume that these visible trends will persist.

On such an assumption, it is far from clear that Britain will, or should, have a smaller population in the year 2000 than it had in the year 1950. It will be noted that this is not the same thing as supposing that Britain will regain its economic supremacy, nor even that there will not be grave economic crises for this country to overcome. But Britain is well placed, both geographically and culturally,

in relation to the world's population densities.   Peaceful
world development along the lines just mentioned almost
unavoidably implies British economic development.

Several of the economic features of the next fifty years
seem likely to work in the direction of preserving the
importance of the urban industrial civilization, which
runs in a great north-west–south-east belt, from Glasgow
and Manchester to Prague.   Air transport brings remote
places near, and so "puts them on the map", but, at the
same time, the easier transport becomes, the greater the
advantages of concentration.   Thus, when steam navi-
gation opened up the Great Lakes and the China coast,
this enhanced, and did not detract from, the growth of
Liverpool, Rotterdam and Hamburg.   When London
Transport extended the possibility of suburban living
deep into the home counties, this did not take activity
away from the vicinity of Piccadilly Circus, but extended
the great wheel of which that Circus is the hub.   So, too,
the industrial and agricultural growth of India, China,
Africa and South America may well bring increased trade
and activity to the skilled industrialists of Western Europe
as well to those of Eastern America.

That is not, of course, a certain outcome of the trend
of economic events, but only a possibility.   It depends
upon, among other factors, the form that the economic
development of overseas areas takes.   Long-distance
transport is, even to-day, the smaller part of total transport; local transport is always denser than long-distance
hauls.   But if the sketch that has been given is even
approximately correct there seems to be no economic-
geographical reason why Britain, granted a favourable
form of rapid world economic development, should not
support an even larger population in A.D. 2000 than
in 1950.

What then of the economic objections, of the "burden" argument, or the balance of payments problem?

The first of these arguments cannot be precisely refuted, because the shapes of all the dynamic functions involved are not known. But it seems likely that a large, and rather wide, capital base will still be essential to the British economy. Britain's survival as an industrial nation demands the adaptation of its industries to extensive changes in the world situation; it starts off on this task with an alarmingly large legacy of obsolescent or even obsolete industrial and domestic buildings and equipment, and social capital. To replace that stock, to increase it, and to make full use of the new replacements may require a larger rather than a smaller working population.

For example, the existence of a building industry of one million operatives is an asset so long as an extensive policy of replacement can be afforded, and is required by demand. Or again, a modernized iron and steel industry, consisting of larger units of production than were common in Britain in the 1930's, needs a large home market if economies arising from high consumption are to be secured.

Those who argue against a rising population on the grounds that it imposes a "burden" on the economy sometimes seem to fear that the country will have too little capital per head, and at others that the labour force will be insufficient to sustain the burden. A situation can indeed be imagined where both factors would be insufficient for any added burden. But the two factors cannot be scarce relatively to each other at the same time. If the "burden" argument, as applied to Britain, is a manpower argument, then it can indeed be seen, from British experience in World War II, that the manpower problem rapidly becomes acute for this country when a great economic burden is imposed, additional to the normal necessity to produce enough for current consumption, and for "normal" capital formation. This provides, however, an argument for an increased, not for a reduced, population in the long run. If the "burden" is the short-run burden of raising children, then immigration ought to be encouraged rather than child-raising. But there are obvious social reasons for not pressing this point to its logical conclusion.

The introduction of highly labour-saving capital appliances might weaken the argument in favour of a higher population, and strengthen the case for a form of economic development that could be attained with a smaller working population. But let us imagine what would be the result if the present factory employed population of Britain [1] attained an output per head double that which it now attains. If it were distributed as at present, surpluses of unsold goods would soon arise; but if it could be suitably re-distributed, some persons perhaps leaving industry altogether for service occupations that cannot be now manned, and some (or all) taking part of their increased real income in the form of increased leisure, the final result could hardly fail to be that the total employed population (factory and non-factory) would rise rather than decline. For there are innumerable unsatisfied needs that could then be satisfied within these islands or abroad.

The true problem then arising would not be so much that of employment as of raw materials and of imports generally. This brings us once more to consider the

[1] The M.O.L. gives a figure of 8,483,000 persons employed in all manufacturing industries (excluding building and contracting, gas, water and electricity, transport, distributive trades and miscellaneous services)—*M.O.L. Gazette*, February 1953.

crucial difficulty; how far the problem of procuring imports is insoluble, and whether it is, as some suppose, the inexorable law of diminishing returns at last restraining the British population from further advance, after, for two centuries, successive exploits of ingenuity have succeeded in resisting that law.

As already noted, this formidable problem is to be thought of as long- rather than as short-term in its effects on population. Sometimes the two kinds of effects have tended to become confused with each other. In the difficult years from 1946 to 1950, the British export drive coincided with a painful recuperation in world agriculture, and, in the same years, Britain had to meet the difficulties created by its violent losses in capital assets at home, at sea and abroad. Calculations to the effect that if population were to be increased by 1 per cent, this would involve a rise of $2\frac{1}{2}$ per cent in *exports*, to pay for the extra imports involved, were made at that time. But the numerical results (they varied between one authority and another) were based on assumptions as to the marginal propensity to import, and the terms of trade, which took no account of any long-term dynamic changes that might be favourable to this country, and the current economic conditions of that period, with its succession of crises, seemed to justify a pessimistic outlook.

A long-term self-denying policy should enable Great Britain to live comfortably with imports limited to only 80 per cent of the quantity imported in 1938. Western German agricultural production, inefficient though it is in output per man compared with British, provides 55 per cent of German bread grain needs, and 95 per cent of its meat requirements (the German diet is of lower high-quality protein value than the British). Even in value terms Western German agricultural production exceeds that of the U.K., although the arable area is not much greater in Western Germany than here.[1]   Again, Western Germany's consumption of motor spirit and diesel oil was about half that of the United Kingdom.   Britain imported three times as great a value of manufactured goods as Western Germany.   The U.K.'s imports are still on the scale that might be expected of a country that had for decades followed a policy of free trade, while Western Germany had the advantages (and, of course, the disadvantages) of an autarchic system built up over a long period, which kept down its standard of living but insulated it from adversities of fluctuating foreign currency balances.

This is not an argument in favour of the U.K. copying the industrial and commercial pattern of autarchic Germany.   But the contrast illustrates the point that Britain could, if pressed, or if the political choice were made, hope to manage on a far lower level of imports than it now deems indispensable.

Furthermore, there are some grounds for hoping that Britain's export prospects are not so dim as is feared. Mr. Tyszynski has indeed shown [2] that, excluding German and Japanese trade, even in 1950 the U.K.'s share of trade had declined in general from 1937, and in 1937 there had already been a heavy fall.   But while he pointed out the seriousness of this trend, he also analysed the main industries in which Britain gained a share from 1937 to 1950, notably agricultural machinery, electrical goods, vehicles and non-ferrous metals, and he, like Professor Phelps-Brown,[3] produced evidence to suggest that Britain's export prices rose less than the world average

---

[1] See *Economic Survey of Europe Since the War*, E.C.E., 1953.
[2] Tyszynski, 1951, p. 6.
[3] Phelps-Brown, 1949.

in 1950 (from pre-war), and that the failure to gain a greater export trade was at least not primarily due to higher relative costs.

The pessimism that suggests that Britain's long-term trading problem is insoluble (that is, that it can never balance its overseas accounts, and must eschew population growth for fear of exacerbating this difficulty) is largely founded on the belief, much publicized for political reasons, that the failure to sell abroad was due solely or mainly to British real wages (or real wages inclusive of social benefits) being out of line with world costs generally. There are two schools of thought on this issue. The extremists of the pessimistic school treat the problem as in effect self-evident.[1] If more exports are not sold prices are too high; wages should therefore be reduced, or the pound devalued as a means to securing the same end. The more moderate of these "classical" thinkers take their stand on the law of comparative costs, as of long-term significance.[2]

The opposing school rests its case upon two factors, the elasticities of demand and supply, and the importance of the income factor rather than the price factor in determining the volume of international trade. They argue that it would be unavailing for Britain to devalue its currency at frequent intervals, and that the solution to the balance of payments problem is an appropriate change in the structure of the British economy. This presumably implies a policy of deliberate reduction in Britain's propensity to import, and an increase in its capacity to export.

The merits of these opposing views cannot be finally resolved. The future population of Great Britain is seen,

[1] See Kent, 1951, and Robbins, 1953.
[2] See Viner, 1953.

however, clearly to depend upon which type of industrial and commercial policy is pursued, and upon how far it is successful. If Britain is to support a larger population, it must succeed in overcoming the obstacles to its exports, both visible and invisible, and in restraining by a cautious policy the volume of the imports it requires.

This is, however, only an incomplete part of the economic problem that faces Britain. The wider problem is none other than that of the development of the backward areas, which means in a practical sense, the development of the whole world. The future population of Britain, like many other results, will depend upon the pattern of investment in many other countries. Mere restrictionism, necessary in some directions, will not solve Britain's balance of payments difficulties. Only if the countries which need investment, either in the direct form of capital goods, or in the indirect form of consumption goods to provide a "wages" fund during a period of build-up, want to obtain these goods from Britain, can this country continue to fulfil a function analogous to that which it has long performed. The size of the future population that Britain can support will be decided not within these islands but on the larger world stage.

§ 6. *Political and Social Pros and Cons.* The relationship of population size to political power is possibly as complex as most other strategic relationships; evidently it would be foolish and naïve to suppose that the most populated countries were the most powerful, yet, on the other hand, there may well be considerable substance in the view that, other things being equal (particularly real incomes per head), the larger political entity exceeds in strength the smaller. The main reason why population alone does not spell power is that the economic link between a potential labour force and an effective production of military material varies in its leverage from one country to another; those with a much higher productivity per head gaining a military potential out of proportion to their size.

French writers have traditionally been aware of the importance of population size for military strength. But they have, perhaps, tended to overlook the importance of what was contained in the "other things equal" qualification to this doctrine. British writers have tended to avoid explicit discussion of the theme. Yet in everyday controversy there is general recognition of the power factor implied by population.

According to the dogmas of a small clique of economists, discussion of these matters is inconsistent with the scientific calling of disciples of the art of which Adam Smith was one of the founders; yet Smith himself emphasized that the first duty of the sovereign was defence, and did not hesitate to discuss the fiscal and economic consequences of this institutional duty and necessity.

In the eighteenth century Gibbon remarked that no state was thought, by the ablest politicians, to be capable of maintaining above 1 per cent of its members "in arms and idleness", which presumably meant that about 2 per cent of the national income was then, in peace-time and at a pinch, available for defence purposes. In the French Wars, Pitt no doubt exceeded this maximum. At the beginning of the twentieth century a figure of 3 per cent was thought to be high, and in 1913 4 per cent represented an unheard-of arms race. The Fascist powers (Germany and Italy) reached 12–14 per cent in the years leading up to World War II. At present the U.S. seems to be spending about 15 per cent of its national income on arms. Evidently the military resources of a nation will depend largely (and for material reasons only, ignoring moral factors) upon the size of its national income, and the degree to which it can tax its resources for such purposes.

Crude population numbers nevertheless still play some part. However severely the strategic rôle of infantry has declined, it remains the arm of final tactical assault, and essential for police purposes and the occupation of hostile territory. A country like Britain, which can raise four and a half millions in the armed forces,[1] carries more weight in the world to-day (just for that reason) than a country like Sweden, with a fighting force perhaps no less efficient man for man, but smaller.

In this section we are concerned with Britain's political power only. Another factor in that power must be how it can be mobilized, and the relation of the mobilized force to the civilian industrial (and, of course, commercial and professional) echelons that support it. Economies of scale become very important in this context, as well as degrees of organization. It seems doubtful whether an island power with much less than 50 millions could have fought a war so effectively as Britain fought World War II; even so, and even with a far more successful mobilization of total manpower than Germany, Britain was outnumbered and outgunned heavily as a European power.

It was observed on theoretical grounds that militarists tended to regard the "optimum" population as some size larger than the economic optimum. This rule seems to apply to Britain, even on the most realistic assumptions. Let it be assumed that Britain has no plan to become a first-class power again, but only to maintain its

[1] In addition to which there were 1·5 millions under arms in the Home Guard.

second-class status, with a potential military strength great enough to secure its alliances, and reasonable treatment from its allies.   Even on this basis, Britain is short of manpower.   In previous wars it had imperial armies on which it could rely to fill this gap.   If the assumption is made that these will no longer be available, then it seems fairly clear that Britain itself would be far stronger militarily if it could maintain a population not of 50 but of 70 or 80 millions.   It might well become dangerously weak militarily if its population fell to 40 or 45 millions, composed predominantly of elderly and middle-aged people.

Should this power diagnosis have any merit (some further arguments in its favour arise from a review of the world situation), it would appear that British population policy, on political grounds, should be directed, if economically possible, to favouring natural increase, *and* at the same time a steady stream of European immigration. On this view, the British economy, and military plan, should be based on a closer link with Europe.   As a nation of 50 millions our strength is not high ; as part of a group of 240 millions (the N.A.T.O. size) or 290 millions (N.A.T.O. plus the sitters on the fence) British–Western European prospects of survival are very high indeed.   What, then, of integrating Britain more closely with Western Europe?

Such a policy implies the freer immigration of Europeans into Britain.   But it does not imply either a failure to develop east-west trade or a weakening of links with the empire.   Such links must be maintained for economic no less than sentimental reasons; and may ultimately strengthen, not weaken, Britain's demographic position as some high-quality dominion citizens return to Britain for their education and even their careers.   A dispassionate review of statistics of exports and of their places of destination readily illustrates the force of this contention.[1]

[1] The following percentages relate to the value of U.K. trade with the Commonwealth in imports, exports and re-exports:

	1913 %	1929 %	1937 %	1949 %
Imports . . .	25	29	39	48
Exports . . .	37	44	48	55
Re-exports . .	13	21	16	—

CHAPTER X

WORLD POPULATION

FOR some other countries, in addition to the U.K., economic factors are likely to predominate in determining their population growth, but to the world as a whole a different argument is perhaps applicable. A large proportion of the world's total population lives under circumstances which have given fuller rein to what are best called demographic impulses.

World population growth, as a whole, has apparently accelerated markedly in recent decades. The consequence is that the world is facing a process which may surpass in importance the "demographic revolution" of the western countries in the last hundred years.[1] The large group of countries with high fertility and considerably lower mortality, a mortality which may decline even more spectacularly in the future than in the past, may quadruple in numbers within fifty years, if there is no emigration. The countries with high mortality as well as high fertility (which include most of the larger countries of Asia and Africa, outside the U.S.S.R.) have yet to feel the impact of medical and sanitary reforms that have reduced death-rates elsewhere. Birth-rates are liable to rise rather than fall in those countries in which a reduced death-rate has resulted in a population with a lower average age than before. While it is admittedly impossible to predict how long the acceleration in the growth of world population will continue, already its accelerated

[1] See *Preliminary Report on the World Social Situation*, U.N., Dept. of Social Affairs, New York, 1952, p. 18.

growth presents large problems, and no end to that growth can yet be seen.

The consequences of this demographic surge will be felt throughout the fifty-year period now under discussion. The half-century to A.D. 2000 can hardly fail to be one in which the numbers on the globe increase at a rate that may outrun the economic organization to support them.

It would be inaccurate to describe this situation as population outrunning the means of subsistence, or to pretend that the current situation necessarily illustrates one instance of an inexorable "tendency" of population to multiply too fast. It would be nearer the truth to suggest that the special demographic circumstances of the world have posed an economic problem which will be extremely difficult to solve, but which is not in principle insoluble.

Since 1913 world population has increased perhaps a little more rapidly than the production of foodstuffs by world agriculture. Such would seem to be the conclusion derivable from the accompanying graph,[1] which is based upon the best statistics available at the moment (those compiled by the League of Nations and the United Nations); but it must be remembered that index numbers of production over such a long period are open to a wide margin of error, and subject to several difficulties of interpretation. An index number for "mining and manufacturing" output, shown on the same graph, rose out of all proportion to the recorded increase in population.

If these index numbers can be taken to represent, very roughly and tentatively, changes of real significance, some very interesting conclusions can be drawn. First, it is obvious that, as might be expected from the perishable

[1] See Diagram VII.

16

nature of foodstuffs, and from the fact that world population as a whole lives above the absolute minimum apart
from local famines, the output of food and the increase
of population have, on the long view, advanced at something like the same rate.   But the output of food has been

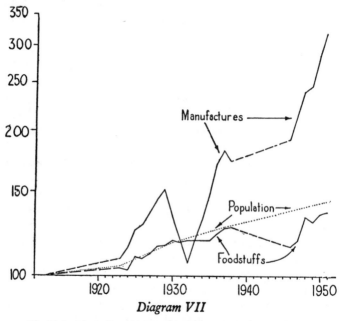

Diagram VII

World trends in Population, Foodstuffs and Manufacturers,
1913–1950 (1913=100)

apparently rather erratic.   It cannot be definitely concluded that it is *more* erratic than changes in population,
since censuses are not taken every year, but it seems very
likely that in peace-time this is so.   There were violent
shifts in population numbers in the war years; but in
those years food production also fluctuated violently.   It
cannot be argued from the trend that population tends

to increase faster than food output. In the late 1920's the curves illustrate the well-known phenomenon of the period of agricultural surpluses. Food output was then tending to rise faster than population. In the world, as then organized politically and economically, the result was a serious crisis, but this was not due to everyone having too much to eat. It was the period of "poverty in the midst of plenty". In World War II there was a staggering reduction in world agricultural output, far greater as a percentage than the temporary drop in population—if it fell at all for the world as a whole. The post-war crisis of balances of payments and continued rationing were largely the consequence of this set-back to world food production.

The overall rate of increase in population being of the order of 1 per cent per annum, it would seem that the world needs to expand its production generally, and its food supply also by a rate of about 1 per cent. This would by no means be a technically insuperable task. The problem is not that of population increasing faster than food supply in this literal sense.

But the food problem of the world is nowadays seen as a problem of nutrition; so that the population problem is a problem not merely of food but of economic and social organization.

§ 1. *The Food Problem.* The nutritional needs of individuals vary, and it cannot be assumed that scientific knowledge of the requirements, even on average, of a consumer is definitive or complete. Vitamin deficiencies are known to exist on an extensive scale in many parts of the world, and, according to current dietetic theory, animal proteins and other essential ingredients of a "protective" diet are especially scarce. Starting from a calculation of needs, the United Nations' experts arrived at much the same conclusion [1] as the F.A.O. reached in 1946. They conclude that to bring the diets of people living in the Far East, the Near East and Africa up, even in a moderate degree, towards an adequate level, would need twice as great a quantity of cereals as are now produced, and much more than twice as much in the way of pulses, meat, milk, eggs and fish. In Latin America and Europe the percentage increase (except for pulses) could be smaller; but even in Oceania and North America, some increase is necessary. But in the Far and Near East, the increase in cereal production since the last world war has only been half that of population, and even in Europe the agricultural recovery has been disappointing.

Thus, the food problem is not in itself a population problem; it is a problem of remedying some of the hopeless malnutrition so long endemic in many parts of the world, and mainly the result of bad organization and of poverty. The remedies which the United Nations' experts suggest (such as the big increase in meat and milk consumption) are not necessarily the most economical, or the most effective, ways of meeting the undoubted dietary deficiencies. The experts' remedies seem indeed to have been thought out more fully from the nutritionist's than from the economist's point of view.

Even in Europe, where birth-rates are falling, and populations beginning to age (although not yet to decline, in general), population increase has outrun food production. The position is unusual. Since 1913 the total population of Europe (excluding the U.S.S.R.) has risen by 21 per cent, but grain production has declined by 5 per cent. Potato production has risen slightly, and sugar-beet production considerably (41 per cent). Total livestock (ex-

[1] *Ibid.*, p. 44.

cluding horses) has risen by 10 per cent, and the horse population has declined by 17 per cent. European agriculture thus seems, as a whole, to have stagnated; although the story for various separate regions and countries of Europe gives a different account of the matter than the European average. What seems to have happened in Europe as a whole is that the increased population has been supported partly by increased imports and partly by the foodstuffs released by the gradual abolition of the horse and other draught animals.

Great political disturbances have ravished European agriculture since 1913, and large shifts in agricultural populations have not improved the ease of management, or the continuity of cultivation. Agricultural land in Europe has been lost, for other purposes, on quite a substantial scale (4·3 million hectares from 1911 to 1938, and a further amount, 2·4 million hectares, from 1938 to 1950). The decline in land use affected grain production most of all, and fallow land; the acreages of permanent grass, industrial crops and potatoes and vegetables all increased over the last fifty years. In 1938 the U.S.S.R. had 102 million hectares sown to grains, about 15 per cent greater than the area of the whole of the rest of Europe put together. Russia before 1914 was, of course, a heavy exporter of grain to Western Europe, supplying about half the needs of that part of the world.

Eastern and Mediterranean Europe have had a rather different production history from that of Western Europe. Territorial changes after both world wars had the effect of progressively shifting surplus grain-producing areas from Western to Eastern Europe. Other particularly adverse factors have affected the twentieth-century development of European agriculture, such as the disturbing effects of two world wars (both of which decreased population to some extent, but food production to an even greater extent) ; of the agricultural depression of the 1930's ; and of the sweeping changes of land tenure in the U.S.S.R. with its initially upsetting consequences.   In a more suitable political and economic atmosphere European agriculture seems to be technically capable of a much more rapid advance than can yet be recorded.   A large-scale flow of agricultural products from the East to the West is a technical possibility, for example, and there are many other ways in which the land resources of Europe as a whole could be far better exploited with existing technical knowledge.

Agricultural statistics make it very noticeable that some of the best agricultural practices, in terms of output per unit of input, the latter measured in units of various factors of production, seem to be obtained in the more industrialized, and more densely populated, countries of Europe.   Thus the yields per cow (expressed in thousands of litres) are highest in the Netherlands, Denmark, Belgium, Switzerland and the United Kingdom.   Professor Dudley Stamp has emphasized the same point by means of an index of agricultural production, which shows yield per acre highest on average for industrialized European countries.

On the world scale, a similar law seems to prevail ; the more industrialized a country, the higher the productivity of its agriculture.   In Japan, for example, rice yield per hectare is more than three times as high as that of India. Diminishing returns in agriculture in the strict technical sense seem to occur here and there, but are the exception rather than the rule.   To increase the use of fertilizer in the world as a whole would more than proportionately increase the yield in tons of food, assuming that all other factors of production were to be held constant ; where agriculture has been "industrialized" yields seem often to have increased more than proportionately to the additional capital invested.

But are there not diminishing returns to labour? The answer to that point is not so certain, for while there seems to be disguised unemployment, and an over-supply of labour in some agricultural areas, in others additional labour could be employed with a more than proportionate increase in the tons of food produced (for example, in areas of not fully exploited land hitherto very lightly and extensively cultivated, or in labour-intensive market gardening not yet pushed to its limits). The net effect of these two opposite forces cannot easily be assessed, but at least it can be said that even strict, non-temporal, diminishing returns apply only to a part of the agricultural industry.

As for diminishing returns in the looser sense, operating over time, and representing returns to changes in the scale of agricultural operations, there seems to be very little reason indeed for supposing that they need come into force for the next few decades, and still less over a fifty-year period. Technological advance is by no means exhausted, or confined to manufacture, nor have existing discoveries all been fully exploited.

But this amounts to a review of the technical rather than of the economic possibilities. There is an additional semi-technical point which bedevils any discussion of the economic forces that affect the chances of realizing that potential increase of food supply that a growing world population will need to keep alive and well. The additional point is that the *distribution*, between countries, of reserve supplies of agricultural land is uneven, and will lead to an unbalance in the balances of payments that the separate countries maintain.

For, as Professor Dudley Stamp has pointed out,[1] the surprising idea has to be accepted that agriculturally speaking the United States is one of the principal under-developed countries of the world.[2]   Despite the high yield per man-hour of its agriculture, its yield per acre is low for a temperate climate, and its conservation, though improving, still inadequate.   Together with the United States, Argentina, Canada and the U.S.S.R. are the countries from which really large increases of food supply could most readily be achieved.   Compared with their immediate potential, the untapped potential of the tropical parts of Africa or other continents is remote and ineffective—so far as present technical knowledge affords any answer.   At best, the tropical areas would require extensive and risky investment, while the extensively farmed areas in temperate climates may well yield increasing returns to quite moderate investment in fertilizer and machinery.

There is very little doubt that sufficient food *can* be produced to meet not only the population growth of another fifty years, but to increase the amount and quality of the food eaten by the larger proportion of the world's inhabitants.   The relevant question arises, however, what economic conditions are necessary for this result to occur?   What stimulus will produce that increase in food supply which nutritionists declare to be desirable?

Two kinds of farming situation reveal high " efficiency "; first, the kinds that prevail in north-western Europe, especially in Denmark and the United Kingdom.   Yield per hectare is high in these countries, where farming is

[1] L. Dudley Stamp, *Land for Tomorrow*, 1952, pp. 114–15.
[2] The U.S.A. is certainly an under-developed area, in a more general sense, if the use of that term preferred by Professor Viner is accepted (see p. 238, below).

mechanized, and the farmers live in close contact with a highly industrialized, and densely populated, urban civilization. Secondly, there is the situation that prevails in the more favoured agricultural regions of China and Japan, where farming is highly efficient in the sense that nothing is allowed to be wasted, and intensive production of small plots of land provides a high level in food raised per hectare, by methods akin to those used in Western market gardening. In both instances there is an economic reason for the kind of agricultural economy that flourishes, the north-western European having to supply food in a region where land is dear, and labour cost rising, but capital goods are relatively cheap, and consumption goods in adequate supply. In these circumstances managerial skill and organization will be well rewarded, for the real incomes of farmers will be kept reasonably high so long as they maintain their output by increasingly capitalistic methods. In China, on the other hand, the pressing need for subsistence, and the absence of cash-crop markets, or a full supply of consumer goods, encourages a system of very small, largely self-sufficient, intensively cultivated family land holdings.

It must not be thought that extensive farming, such as is practised in the U.S.A. or Canada, is necessarily inefficient (except where it is accompanied by bad farming methods leading to soil erosion), for extensive farming, too, largely originates from the economic situation of the prairie farmers, with plentiful land, dear labour and distant markets to serve. But it is wasteful in its use of land, and therefore it is wasteful of an important scarce resource, so far as world population presses upon land resources (or nutritional need results in such pressure).

Nutritional need is not the same thing as economic demand. From a population point of view the raising of

nutritional standards is essential. For population growth
to slow down, and cease to be determined largely by blind
urges, it is necessary that standards of living should rise;
and if these rise, it follows that nutritional needs will
become better satisfied. For those needs are among the
most urgent demands that men with money to spend will
make upon the economic system. The prospects of
raising the economic living standards of the world are
directly relevant therefore to the question whether or not
population pressures will be alleviated.

§ 2. *Economic Prospects.* It cannot be said that, apart
from the neo-Malthusians and the neo-Godwinians mentioned in an earlier chapter, there are many economists
willing to risk their reputations upon a sketch of the
future course of world economic development and hence
of world population; a subject to which, however, it is
now most relevant to address ourselves.

Food supplies have already been discussed; we now
have to consider what type of economic development is
necessary to secure that food. Is the distribution of
economic activity, and of incomes, throughout the world
going to be consistent with the bringing to market of the
necessary supplies? Are other kinds of shortage going
to restrain the growth of population by imposing unpleasant forms of check to the increasing means of subsistence? Will the world's population be halted by
shortages of clothing or shelter, or drugs, or raw materials,
or by diseases particular to overcrowding?

The economic prospects of the world are determined
not merely by the amount of its wealth, and the size of
its real income, but by the distribution of these quantities.
For it is by the offer of a distribution of wealth or income
that men àre induced, for the most part, to work and

produce more wealth or more income, though in some important instances, it is true, they work for quite different motives.

Incomes are distributed throughout the world in a very uneven manner, and a tendency has been at work to even out some of the international differences of income, just as there has been a movement within countries to alleviate the discrepancies between the purchasing power of different individuals or classes. This "tendency" or "movement", vaguely or deliberately towards more egalitarian income distribution, has been counteracted by powerful and impersonal (as well as personal) economic forces with a quite opposite or reactionary tendency. Greater economic power has accumulated in the hands of a few powerful people, and been used further to increase the differences of income.

The net result has been, so far, some increase in equality. But, even within a single country, this increase does not necessarily please all classes, or indeed even any particular class. For, supposing there are, say, three classes in a community, A, B and C, with average incomes of £x, £y and £z respectively, it would be an egalitarian measure to increase the number of people in class B by diminishing the number in class C. But if this were done on a large scale the average *income* of class B might be less than £y after the change, so that even though greater equality of income was achieved, and greater average income for the community as a whole, the average income of *each class* might quite conceivably fall. But, though many, perhaps a majority, would have higher incomes, some would necessarily have lower incomes, and each class might have, on average, a lower income. People tend to identify status with income, and even though thousands more may become doctors and professional men, skilled artisans instead of unskilled workers, and so on, they may judge themselves ill-used after the change because they can no longer expect so high an income as someone in their (new) class could have expected before the change.

Greater equality is practically impossible to attain unless the average incomes of each class can be reduced. So it is an unspoken, and politically unpopular, objective of any egalitarian policy to *reduce* the average income of nearly every class in the community, so as to *raise* the average income of the community as a whole.[1] The two objectives of greater equality, and of increased overall average real income per head, are almost inevitably accompanied by reduced average class income per head, the reason being that the first two objectives are attained most easily by raising people from the lower to the higher classes.

If this reasoning is applied to international affairs, it will be seen how difficult it will be for the nutritionists' ideals to be realized without conflict and friction.   Voices are already being raised to protest against the consequences of increased egalitarianism.

Some writers seem to think [2] that there has *not* been any progress towards a rise in real *per capita* income in the world since 1913, because only a small, and shrinking, proportion of world population has had a rapid increase in its standard of living, and the rest of the world has had only a slight increase, or remained stationary.   Nevertheless, the median world income has almost certainly declined, and this is wrongly supposed to imply that there

[1] This is a secondary but important objective of some egalitarian policies, the idea being to increase productivity by offering individuals better chances of rising from class C to class B; and also to take advantage of technological opportunities at a more rapid rate than would be tolerated if this alleviation were not offered to those who originally composed class C.

[2] See Singer, 1949, p. 1.

has not been a rise in income, and that there has not been an increase in equality.

A fall in median income is not inconsistent with either of these results; in fact, it has been already conceded that real incomes have everywhere risen or stayed stationary.

It is important to realize that the slow rise to greater real incomes of the enormous hordes of poor people in the world would possibly reduce some of the real incomes of those now much more fortunate, and would almost certainly reduce the *average* of each social or economic group's real income, into which groups some of the backward peoples of the world succeeded in penetrating. If they become textile workers in their thousands, textile wages may fall; if they become coal-miners, coal prices may decline. Organized labour in the more advanced countries has long been frightened by this possibility, and has sought, in capitalist countries, to protect its members' interests by restrictions on migration and the support of monopolistic enterprise.

Furthermore, those living in countries usually classified as under-developed have also been living in economies mainly supported by the production of primary raw materials or agricultural products (cash crops for food or industrial use); these classes of product have usually been produced under much more competitive conditions than some of the principal products of the more advanced countries. For this, and other reasons, the quantum of manufactured products obtainable for a given quantum of primary goods declined steeply from 1913 to 1939, as Dr. Singer points out,[1] by something like 40 per cent. This shift in the terms of trade against the interests of the primary producers has led their leaders to look very sceptically at plans to keep them primary.

[1] *Ibid.*, p. 5.

From their point of view, increases in efficiency in the production of primary products have mainly been passed on to the customer.   Increasing returns are of no avail to them, for they produce competitively for a market with an inelastic demand and lose when production is high. Their trading terms deteriorate, and their customers gain all, or more than all, the advantage of new methods. Their main objective is, therefore, to secure by hook or by crook a more rapid industrial development, and both to import and to make more capital goods.

What is an under-developed country, and what types of country are classified, in United Nations documents for example, as under-developed?   Varying definitions are given, but this seems to be because the line between "developed" and "under-developed" countries has to be drawn arbitrarily for any particular purpose, rather than because of uncertainty as to the general meaning of the term.   Under-developed means, in general usage, poor countries, those with relatively low real *per capita* income, and the term is no doubt a euphemism, like the term under-privileged.[1]   One major economic problem of the world is precisely the fact, moreover, that the under-developed (poor) countries are not necessarily so profitable to develop, or so "ripe for development" whatever the system of profits in force, as are some of the already industrialized countries.

The economic conditions necessary to secure food and

[1] Professor Viner, in a full discussion of the word, has pointed out the difficulty of equating "under-developed" with low ratio of population to area, or countries with high interest rates, or ratio of capital to other factors, or ratio of industrial output to total output, or "young" *versus* "old"; but having knocked down these Aunt Sallies to his satisfaction he suggests that countries with good prospects of using more factors of production are to be called under-developed.   This makes the term useless for ordinary speech, as the principal under-developed countries in the world would then probably be the U.S.A. and Canada. (See Viner, 1953, pp. 94–8.)

other requirements of the increasing population of the world are, therefore, to be defined in terms of deliberate policies, rather than of natural forces. This is not a veiled way of hinting that all major economic activities should be regimented or planned in detail; it is instead a conclusion that seems to follow from the facts of to-day, and it amounts to stating that some degree of international economic planning is necessary, unless population increase is to lead to international disaster. The "natural forces" of ordinary greed and selfishness would lead to increased investment in advanced countries, extended monopolistic and perhaps military power exercised by citizens of a few leading countries over the rest of the inhabitants of the world, and gross economic exploitation of the peoples of the backward areas, as a source of cheap labour. This policy would in the long run be likely to fail for economic as well as for political reasons, but might succeed for a fairly long "short run".

International economic planning may be assumed over the next few decades to be at a minimum; this seems a more likely assumption than the more optimistic assumptions often made when the United Nations Charter was drafted, and in the immediately succeeding years. Experience has shown that the international lending of dollars on a large scale is unlikely, but that, from time to time, the United States is prepared politically to make gifts to other nations. Policies for the next fifty years must take account of a continuing dollar gap tending to recur, since America's propensity to export is so much stronger than its propensity to import, and a flow of lending, or gold, to balance the accounts will not be available.

In this situation, the under-developed countries will undoubtedly be found trying to finance their own capital development, by squeezing a surplus for investment out of their own inhabitants. Britain industrialized itself from its own capital resources, and the newly industrializing countries will most likely aim at following along the same hard path. By this means they will aim at creating the flow of capital and consumers' goods locally, which will form the real offer that they can make to their agriculturalists to induce them to increase their supplies; and similarly to their suppliers of buildings, clothing and other necessities. To a large extent they will pull themselves up by their own bootstraps, though welcoming any economic help from abroad that is offered on politically acceptable terms.

The future offers *either* a period of more intensive imperialist exploitation *or* a system of joint investment by the under-developed countries themselves and the advanced countries, the share of the former in their own development becoming larger than is often anticipated. There are many serious political difficulties in the way of the second of these two possibilities, arising not only from the world struggle for power but from the internal social structure of most of the under-developed countries, which is often ill-adapted for encouraging substantial economic development.

Supposing that all these internal political difficulties can be overcome (an uncertain hypothesis), there will still remain the problem of deciding what types of investment should be encouraged first in the under-developed countries. If the U.S.A., Canada, Argentina, Eastern Europe and Russia are to supply most of the increase in basic food, investment in less-developed countries than these should partly be directed to supplying other foodstuffs, and all other types of services and of manufactured articles, that can be sold in the food-producing areas; the less-developed countries will also see some economic advantage in producing manufactured goods for their own home markets. (It will be difficult for Professor Viner to convince them that the U.S.A. succeeded industrially *despite* its commercial policies.)

If the less-developed countries follow mildly protectionist policies (they have already gone a long way in this direction), there will arise a danger of the overdevelopment of certain closely competing types of plant, equipment and skills.

A further major problem as to the type of investment to encourage in an under-developed country is directly related to population increase. If capital equipment is installed in, say, India, which needs labour during its process of construction, this may take into employment thousands of workers who would otherwise be raising food, more or less effectively, on the land.[1] If they are taken off the land long enough, others, owing to the high birth-rate, will replace them, and, should the construction eventually come to an end, the constructional workers will become as redundant as the Irish navvies became when railway building in Britain ceased.

Something depends upon how far the workers drawn into constructional or, later, industrial employment react to their new environment. If they acquire a higher standard of life and at the same time adopt methods of family limitation, there may be some net benefit to a country faced with a serious demographic problem. But if they are employed at real wages not much higher than they would make on the land, their habits may not change, and the situation will grow worse again unless constantly increasing injections of capital can be made to the

[1] This is a reasonable assumption in view of the high percentage at present engaged in agriculture.

17

economy. The only alleviating influence will be the increased real income for the country as a whole, which will presumably result from the use of the capital goods when completed.

If, however, some highly mechanized form of equipment is installed (say, earth-moving machinery that will do the work of hundreds of manual workers), this will provide the service of the capital goods perhaps not more cheaply, but more expeditiously, and with less social disturbance. For instead of two hundred workers being taken from the land, and used in unskilled work, only three or four men may now be required, to receive training and act as crew to the machine. There will be no large secondary increase in population, and the national income of the country will rise more rapidly than any induced population change.

If this argument is correct, there is something to be said for the apparent paradox, that it is better to install, in certain instances, labour-saving capital into under-developed and heavily populated countries, despite the cheapness of the labour on the spot. Britain's nineteenth-century industrial revolution began, after all, with a small population, and took the form of the creation of numerous small workshops, as well as of a few large enterprises. That revolution was also accompanied by, or to some extent preceded by, a revolution in agriculture. The growing towns provided more and more opportunities for work, and larger markets, together with what are now, and were then, thought to have been miserable social conditions.

Countries like India start from a different position in that they already have very large populations. They, too, will need numerous small workshops, employing a rather low amount of capital per head, to employ their large, and demographically growing, population. Such workshops, and primitive small factories, are springing up in their thousands all over the world; and if small machine-tools are supplied to these workers, the world will soon see a prodigious increase in the goods supplied to the world markets. The suggestion made here is not that this kind of development is wrong—it is, indeed, inevitable—but that it should be supplemented, where possible, by the provision of large heavy equipment, at strategic points in the backward economies, regardless of whether or not such equipment is labour-saving.

For example, fertilizer plant, irrigation, power lines and transport facilities are all types of investment that spring to mind as needing to be done mainly on a large scale, although even these kinds of investment can sometimes be partly carried out on more primitive lines. Heavy items of "indivisible" expenditure are often not suitable for piecemeal construction, even where labour is plentiful; their economy of scale is gained in use rather than in being made. This is especially true of transport facilities, which, more than any other kind of social capital, played a major rôle in the economic development of Britain,[1] and will no doubt play a similar rôle in China, India, Africa and South America.

Design of the heavy capital equipment to be installed should, however, take account of the population situation, and of the high degree of disguised unemployment prevailing in the backward countries. A form of transport equipment that would "permanently" (i.e., until wholly replaced or renewed) need a large labour force to maintain it might be appropriate in an under-developed country even though too costly in maintenance to install in an advanced country with high real wages. Any such

[1] Marshall, 1899, pp. 331-2.

choice of labour-using designs must be exercised with care, as labour costs may rise in the under-developed areas quite rapidly as capital, of various types, becomes available to the working population.

The choice of policy for the under-developed countries is not between industrialization and more intensive agricultural development. So long as the world is organized into separate, more or less sovereign, political entities, no country will accept the rôle of being a mere agricultural provider, although as Denmark has shown, that rôle can be both technically advanced and profitable. But even Denmark has had to encourage officially industry as well as agriculture, owing to the fact that its agriculture is exposed to world competition, and reliance on that activity alone is thus dangerous.

The true choice is between one kind or another of industrialization; for the rest, the development of agriculture is dependent upon the development of industry "at home",[1] as well as upon the country's attractiveness as a depository for foreign investment. Agriculturists need markets near at hand, for the most part, as the long haul of food across the oceans must be regarded as exceptional, and the development of towns and cities in backward areas is a necessary complement to the rise in agricultural output needed.

The Indian peasant who produces very little surplus under current conditions, fails to manure his land, or even to work all the hours that he could, is not merely backward; he is responding to an economic environment of poverty. If he produced a surplus over his own and his immediate neighbours' needs, that surplus could probably not be sold. The millions who starve in famines lack

[1] I.e., in whichever under-developed country the argument is applied.

often any purchasing power, and cannot earn anything in current conditions. The problem of poverty has to be met, as it had in nineteenth-century Britain, partly by industrialization; what that cannot cure will form a remaining social problem to be dealt with as such. A discussion of this aspect of the problem would take us too far afield; it may at least be said that social services to relieve unavoidable poverty are already necessary, and have already been partly inaugurated.

§ 3. *Social Changes.* Extensive social changes, as well as economic, may be required before the world population problem assumes a more manageable size. Rapid population growth in countries like India, often exposed to famine, is unfortunately a serious handicap to the social changes, and to the economic development, from which together an economic advance is to be expected.[1] This is the consequence of a vicious circle led by a demographic upsurge, leading back through an economic difficulty to yet a further demographic increase.

To believe this is not to believe in the inevitability of the sequence perpetuating itself, or still less in the view that India, or any other part of the world, is in some absolute sense over-populated. The vicious circle can be summed up in the general statement that, with few exceptions, the countries in which a high proportion of people are engaged in agriculture are also countries where real incomes are relatively low, where nutrition is poor, and where there exist serious cultural as well as economic barriers to agricultural expansion.[2] The danger of this vicious circle is that as labour becomes very cheap in relation to other means of production the circle will never be broken.

[1] See Hajnal, 1952, p. 304.   [2] See Taeuber, C., 1950, pp. 75–6.

But investment of two distinct types, labour-replacing and labour-cooperative, if judiciously selected, may serve to break the circle.

At what pace industrial development will proceed, and at what pace it will have any effect upon the high birth-rates of different social classes, is not known, nor is arm-chair speculation on these points of much value. The basic research has not been done whereby even the past influences of changed economic conditions upon birth-rates could be established, so that there is little upon which to base views as to the future.

In every part of the world research workers are seeking to discover more precisely the factors of all types that affect demographic change, and administrators and technicians are seeking to initiate or sponsor those medical and industrial changes that are favourable to a better life for the poor, in continents where poverty has never been uncommon. It is not known how soon, or even whether for certain, an increased standard of living will result in a more controlled birth-rate, but it is known that without such an increase the birth-rate will remain uncontrolled.

The work of the devoted international civil servants, of the technicians whose salaries are financed by various international bodies, and of the civil servants and indus-trialists of the under-developed countries themselves, is probably inadequate in scale, and ought to be increased in scope. It represents the most serious attempt yet made to meet the problem of world economic develop-ment in an orderly, humane and rational way. Perhaps this work will secure greater and more popular support from the countries with some economic surplus over their needs, as the severity of the population crisis of the half-century ahead forces itself more and more to be recog-nized; for, although there seems to be no insuperable economic difficulty to prevent the world from weathering this great demographic storm, to get through it will demand a large part of the energies of peoples and governments the world over. For this reason, as well as for others not within our scope, the current preoccupation of statesmen with the problem of power in its crudest sense seems to be especially unfortunate; population pressure will almost certainly become so important, within a few decades, as to form the main preoccupation of whoever find themselves in the rôle of the ultimate peacemakers of this century.

BIBLIOGRAPHY

ABRAMS, MARK, *The Population of Great Britain*, Allen & Unwin, London, 1945.

ADAMS, WILLIAM FORBES, *Ireland and Irish Emigration to the New World from 1815 to the Famine*, Yale University Press, 1932.

BARKER, DUDLEY, *People for the Commonwealth; the Case for Mass Migration*, T. W. Laurie, London, 1948.

BAUER, P. T., and YAMEY, B. S., "Economic Progress and Occupational Distribution", *Economic Journal*, Vol. XLI, 1951.

BERTRAM, J. C. L., "Population Trends and the World Biological Resources" in *New Compass of the World*, 1949.

BEVERIDGE, Sir W., "Population and Unemployment", *Economic Journal*, December, 1923.

BLACK, JOHN D., "*Coming Re-adjustments in Agriculture . . .*", *Journal of Farm Economics*, 31 (1, Part 1), 1–15, February, 1949.

—— and Kiefer, Maxine E., *Future Food and Agriculture Policy; a Program for the Next Ten Years*, McGraw Hill Book Co., New York, 1948.

BOIARSKI, A., "Certain Aspects of the Population Problem", [*Soviet*] *News*, December, 1951.

BOURGEOIS-PICHAT, M., in *Economic Survey of Europe since the War*, E.C.E., Geneva, 1953.

BOWEN, I., "Note on the Report of the Economics Committee", *Yorkshire Bulletin of Economic and Social Research*, Vol. 2, No. 2, July, 1950.

BOWLEY, A. L., "Births and Population in Great Britain", *Economic Journal*, Vol. XXXIV, 1924.

BROWN, A. J., *Applied Economics*, Allen & Unwin Ltd., 1947.

BUER, MABEL C., *The Historical Setting of the Malthusian Controversy*, London Essays in Economics in Honour of Edwin Cannan, Routledge & Sons, 1927.

CANNAN, EDWIN, *Elementary Political Economy*, 1888.

——, *A History of the Theories of Production and Distribution in English Political Economy from 1776 to 1848*, 3rd Edition, P. S. King & Son, Ltd., Westminster, 1924.

——, *Wealth*, 3rd Edition, 1928.

——, "The Changed Outlook in regard to Population 1831–1931", *Economic Journal*, Vol. XLI, p. 519, December, 1931.

CANTILLON, RICHARD, *Essai sur la nature du commerce en général*, Londres, Fletcher Gyles dans Holborn, 1755 (reprinted London, Macmillan, 1931).

CARROTHERS, W. A., *Emigration from the British Isles*, P. S. King & Sons, 1929.

CARR-SAUNDERS, A. M., *Population*, Oxford University Press, 1925.

Census 1951, England and Wales, Preliminary Report, H.M.S.O., 1951.

Census 1951, Great Britain, One Per Cent Sample Tables.

Census of Scotland, 1951, H.M.S.O., Edinburgh.

CHANG, PEI-KANG, *Agriculture and Industrialization*, Harvard University Press, Cambridge, Mass., 1949.

CLARK, COLIN, *Conditions of Economic Progress*, 1st Edition, 1940; 2nd Edition, 1951.

CLARK, F. LE GROS, and PIRIE, N. W. (Ed.), *Four Thousand Million Mouths*, Oxford University Press, London, 1951.

CONNELL, K. H., *The Population of Ireland, 1750–1845*, Clarendon Press, Oxford, 1950.

COOK, R. C., *Human Fertility*, Gollancz, London, 1951.

COX, PETER R., "Estimating the Future Population", *Applied Statistics*, Vol. 1, No. 2, June, 1952.

DALTON, H., "The Theory of Population", *Economica*, Vol. VIII, 1928.

DARWIN, CHARLES GALTON, *The Next Million Years*, Rupert Hart-Davies, London, 1952.

DAVIS, J. S., "Our Changed Population Outlook", *American Economic Review*, Vol. XLII, No. 3, June, 1952.

DE CASTRO, JOSUE, *Geography of Hunger*, Gollancz, London, 1952.

DODD, N. E., *The Listener*, Vol. XLVII, No. 1212, May 22, 1952.

EISNER, R., "Under-Employment Equilibrium Rates of Growth", *American Economic Review*, March, 1952.

ELLIS, HOWARD S., *Survey of Contemporary Economics*, Blakiston, 1948.

——, *Readings in Business Cycle Theory*, Allen & Unwin, London, Vol. II of Blakiston Series of republished articles on Economics; Chairman for Vol. II, Gottfried Haberler. First published in Great Britain, 1950.

FELLNER, WILLIAM, *Monetary Policies and Full Employment*, University of California Press, Berkeley, Los Angeles, 1946.

FERENCZI, IMRE, *The Synthetic Optimum of Population*, International Institute of Intellectual Co-operation, League of Nations, Paris, 1938.

——, "Migrations (Modern)", *Encyclopædia of Social Sciences*, Vol. 10, 1933.

—— and WILLCOX, W. F., *International Migration*, Vol. I, *Statistics*, International Labour Office, Bureau of Economic Research, 1929.

FIELD, J. A., *Essays on Population and Other Papers*, University of Chicago Press, 1931.

FOOD AND AGRICULTURAL ORGANIZATION, UNITED NATIONS, Yearbooks.

——, *The State of Food and Agriculture*, 1948 and later years.

FORD, C. S., and BEACH, F. A., *Patterns of Sexual Behaviour*, Eyre and Spottiswoode, 1952.

FORSYTH, WILLIAM D., *The Myth of the Open Spaces*, Melbourne University Press, Melbourne, 1942.

GLASS, D. V., *The Struggle for Population*, Clarendon Press, Oxford, 1936.

——, (Ed.), *An Introduction to Malthus*, Watts, London, 1953.

——, "Population and Family Limitation", *The Listener*, Vol. L, No. 1274, July 30, 1953.

GODWIN, WILLIAM, *Of Population. An Enquiry concerning the Power of Increase in the Numbers of Mankind, being an answer to Mr. Malthus's essay on that subject*, Longman, Hurst, Rees, Orme & Brown, Paternoster Row, London, 1820.

HAJNAL, J., Review of M. Pierre George's "Introduction", 1951, in *Milbank Memorial Fund Quarterly*, Vol. XXX, No. 3, July, 1952.

HANSEN, A. H., "Economic Progress and Declining Population Growth", *American Economic Review*, 1939.

——, *Business Cycles and National Income*, W. W. Norton & Co., Inc., New York, 1951.

HANSEN, MARCUS LEE, *The Atlantic Migration, 1607–1860*, Harvard University Press, Cambridge, Mass., 1940.

HARROD, ROY F., Memorandum submitted in 1944 to the Royal Commission on Population (*q.v.*), reprinted as "The Population Problem" in *Economic Essays*, Macmillan & Co., Ltd., London, 1952.

——, *Towards a Dynamic Economics*, Macmillan & Co., Ltd., London, 1948.

HICKS, J. R., *Value and Capital*, Clarendon Press, Oxford (2nd Edition), 1946.

HIGGINS, BENJAMIN, "Concepts and Criteria of Secular Stagnation", from *Essays in Honour of Alvin Hansen*, New York, 1948.

——, "The Doctrine of Economic Maturity", *American Economic Review*, March, 1946.

—— "The Theory of Increasing Under-Employment", *Economic Journal*, June, 1950.

HILL, A. V., "The Ethical Dilemma of Science", Address to the British Association in the *Advancement of Science*, Vol. IX, No. 34, 1952.

H.M.S.O., Colonial Report: *Mauritius, 1951*, pub. 1952.

HUBBACK, EVA M., *The Population of Great Britain*, Penguin Books, 1947.

ISAAC, JULIUS, "International Migration and European Population Trends", *International Labour Review*, Vol. XLVI, No. 3, September, 1952.

JEFFERSON, MARK, "Distribution of the World's City Folks", *Geographical Review*, Vol. 21, 1931.

KENT, T. W., "1947 Comes Again", *Lloyds Bank Review*, October, 1951.

KEYNES, J. M., *The Economic Consequences of the Peace*, Macmillan, London, 1920.

——, "A Reply to Sir W. Beveridge", *Economic Journal*, December, 1923.

——, "Some Economic Consequences of a Declining Population", *Eugenics Review*, Vol. XXXIX, April, 1937.

KONDRATIEFF, N. D., *Review of Economic Statistics*, Vol. XVII, No. 6, p. 105, November, 1935, and reprinted in *Readings in Business Cycle Theory*, H. S. Ellis, Allen & Unwin, 1950.

LEAGUE OF NATIONS, *Industrialization and Foreign Trade*, U.S.A., 1945.

LEONE, ENRICO DE, "The Distribution of People on the Earth and the Euro-African Problem", *Idea*, Rome, June, 1951.

LORWIN, L. L., and BLAIR, J. M., *Technology in Our Economy*, Monograph No. 22, Temporary National Economic Committee, 1941.

MACDOUGALL, G. D. A., "Britain's Foreign Trade Problem", *Economic Journal*, March, 1947.

MCCLEARY, G. F., *The Malthusian Population Theory*, London, 1953.

MCGREGOR, D. H., *Economic Thought and Policy*, Oxford University Press, 1949.

MALTHUS, T. R., *First Essay on Population*, London, 1798; 2nd ed. 1803.

——, *Principles of Political Economy*, London, 1820.

——, Article on "Population", Supplement to the fourth, fifth and sixth editions *Encyclopædia Britannica*, 1824.

MARSHALL, ALFRED, *Economics of Industry*, 3rd Edition, 1899.

——, *Principles*, 8th Edition, 1938.

MATERIALS POLICY COMMISSION, *Resources for Freedom*, Vols. I–V, Report to the President, United States Government Printing Office, Washington, June, 1952.

MEEK, R. L., *Marx and Engels on Malthus*, Lawrence and Wishart, London, 1953.

MILLS, F. C., "Economic Growth in the United States", *American Economic Review*, 1951.

Ministry of Labour Gazette—Numbers Employed in Great Britain: Industrial Analysis, February, 1953.

MOULTON, H. G., *Controlling Factors in Economic Development*, Brookings Institute, Washington, 1949.

MUMFORD, LEWIS, *Technics and Civilisation*, London, 1946.

NOTESTEIN, F. W., *Population—The Long View*, The Harris Memorial Foundation Lectures, Chicago, 1945.

——, Review of Report of Royal Commission on Population (British) in *Population Studies*, Vol. 3, No. 3, December, 1949.

—— and others, *The Future Population of Europe and the Soviet Union*, League of Nations, Geneva, 1944.

OSBORN, FREDERICK, "Possible Effects of Differential Fertility on Genetic Endowment", Address to the American Eugenics Society, reported in *Population Index*, Vol. 18, No. 3, July, 1952.

PAN CHIA-LIN, Article with I. B. TAEUBER, "The Expansion of the Chinese North and West", *Population Index*, Vol. 18, No. 2, April, 1952, Office of Population Research, Princeton University.

PEARL, R., *The Biology of Population Growth*, Johns Hopkins University Press, Baltimore, 1925.

PENROSE, L. S., *The Biology of Mental Defect*, London, 1949.

PHELPS BROWN, E. H., "Wage Levels after Two Wars", *Westminster Bank Review*, November, 1949.

——, and HANDFIELD-JONES, S. J., "The Climacteric of the 1890's: A Study in the Expanding Economy", *Oxford Economic Papers*, New Series, Vol. 4, No. 3, October, 1952.

PLANT, G. F. (C.B.E.), *Oversea Settlement*, Oxford University Press, London, 1951.

POLITICAL AND ECONOMIC PLANNING, *Population Policy in Great Britain*, London, April, 1948.

Quantitative Inheritance, Papers read at a Colloquium held at the Institute of Animal Genetics, Edinburgh University, under the auspices of the Agricultural Research Council, April 4–6, 1950, H.M.S.O., London, 1952.

RADHAKRISHNAN, Dr. S., "Planned Parenthood", an Address to a conference on planned parenthood, printed in *Eugenics Review*, Vol. 45, No. 1, April, 1953.

RAVENSTEIN, E. G., "The Laws of Migration", *Journal of the Royal Statistical Society*, Vol. XLVIII, 1885.

REDDAWAY, W. B., *The Economics of a Declining Population*, Allen & Unwin, London, 1939.

Registrar-General's Statistical Review, 1950.

REINHARD, M. R., *Histoire de la Population Mondiale, de 1700 à 1948*, Editions Domat-Montchrestien, [1949].

ROBBINS, LIONEL, *The Optimum Theory of Population*, London Essays in Economics in Honour of Edwin Cannan, Routledge & Sons, 1927.

——, "Notes on Some Probable Consequences of the Advent of a Stationary Population in Great Britain", *Economica*, Vol. IX, 1929.

——, "Certain Aspects of the Theory of Costs", *Economic Journal*, March, 1934.

——, *The Economic Basis of Class Conflict*, Macmillan, London, 1939.

——, *The Theory of Economic Policy in English Classical Political Economy*, Macmillan, London, 1952.

——, "The International Economic Problem", *Lloyds Bank Review*, January, 1953.

ROBINSON, AUSTIN, "The Future of British Imports", *The Three Banks Review*, No. 17, March, 1953.

ROBINSON, JOAN, "The Model of the Expanding Economy", *Economic Journal*, Vol. LXII, No. 245, March, 1952.

ROBERTS, MICHAEL, *The Estate of Man*, Faber & Faber, 1951.

RODWAY, A. E. (Ed.), *Godwin and the Age of Transition*, Harrap & Son, 1952.

ROYAL COMMISSION ON POPULATION, Selected Papers, 1949–50.

——, Report, Cmd. 7695, H.M.S.O., 1949.

SALTER, ROBERT M., "World Soil and Fertilizer Resources in Relation to Food Needs", *Science* (published by the American Association for the Advancement of Science), Vol. 105, January–June, 1947.

SAMUELSON, P. A., *Economics: An Introductory Analysis*, McGraw Hill Book Co., Inc., New York, 1948.

SAUVY, ALFRED, "Some Aspects of the International Migration Problem", *International Labour Review*, Vol. LVIII, No. 1, July, 1948.

——, *Théorie Générale de la Population*, Vol. 1, *Economie et Population*, Presses Universitaires de France, 1952.

——, "Productivité, Production, Population optimum, Application à l'Europe occidentale", *Population—Revue Trimestrielle*, janv.–mars, 1952, Institut National d'Etudes Demographiques, Paris.

SCHUMPETER, JOSEPH A., "Analysis of Economic Change", *Review of Economic Statistics*, Vol. XVII, No. 4, May, 1935.

——, *Capitalism, Socialism and Democracy*, London, 1943.

SCHMOOKLER, JACOB, "The Changing Efficiency of the American Economy, 1869–1938", *Review of Economics and Statistics*, Vol. XXXIV, No. 3, August, 1952.

Scott Committee, *Land Utilisation in Rural Areas*, Cmd. 6378, August, 1942.

Singer, H. W., "Economic Progress in Under-developed Countries", *Social Research*, Vol. 16, 1949.

Smith, J. Russell, "Science, New Machinery and the Population of Asia", *New Compass of the World*, by Weigert, Stefansson and Harrison, London, 1949.

Smith, Kenneth, *The Malthusian Controversy*, London, 1951.

Snyder, Carl, "Capital Supply and National Well-being", *American Economic Review*, June, 1936.

Spengler, Joseph J., *French Predecessors of Malthus*, Duke University Press, Durham, North Carolina, 1942.

——, "The World's Hunger—Malthus 1948", *Proceedings of the Academy of Political Science*, 23 (2): 53–71, January, 1949.

Sraffa, P. (Ed.), *The Works and Correspondence of David Ricardo* C.U.P., 1951.

Stamp, D. L., *Land of Britain*, London, 1948.

——, *Land for Tomorrow, the Under-Developed World*, American Geographical Society, Indiana University Press, 1952 (published in Britain by Faber & Faber as *Our Undeveloped World*, 1953).

Steuart, Sir James, *An Inquiry into the Principles of Political Œconomy—being an essay on the Science of Domestic Policy in Free Nations*, Vols. I and II, London, 1767.

Stewart, John Q., "Empirical Mathematical Rules Concerning the Distribution and Equilibrium of Population", *Geographical Review*, Vol. 37, 1947.

Stigler, George J., "The Ricardian Theory of Value and Distribution", *Journal of Political Economy*, Vol. LX, No. 3, June, 1952.

Stix, R. K., "Contraceptive Service in Three Areas", *Milbank Memorial Fund Quarterly*, Vol. XIX, Nos. 2 and 3, April and July, 1941.

Stone, R., "The Fortune Teller", *Economica*, February, 1943.

Swaroop, S., *Growth of Population in the World*, World Health Organisation, Epidemiological and Vital Statistics Report, Vol. 4, April, 1951.

Sweezy, Paul, "Declining Investment Opportunity", Ch. 32 of *The New Economics*, ed. by S. E. Harris, London, 1948.

——, "On Secular Stagnation" from *Post-War Economic Problems*, ed. S. E. Harris, 1943.

Taeuber, Conrad, "Utilisation of Human Resources in Agriculture", *Milbank Memorial Fund Quarterly*, Vol. XXXVII, No. 1, January, 1950.

Taeuber, Irene B., "Ceylon as a Demographic Laboratory; Preface to Analysis", *Population Index*, October, 1949.

TERBORGH, GEORGE, *The Bogey of Economic Maturity*, Chicago, 1945.

THOMAS, BRINLEY, "Migration and the Rhythm of Economic Growth, 1830–1913", *Manchester School of Economic and Social Studies*, Vol. XIX, 1951.

TIZARD, Sir HENRY, Address to British Association, 1948, *Advancement of Science*, Vol. V, No. 19.

TRIANTIS, S. G., "Economic Progress, Occupational Redistribution and International Terms of Trade", *Economic Journal*, September, 1953.

TYSZYNSKI, H., "World Trade in Manufactured Commodities 1899–1950", *Manchester School, etc.*, Vol. XIX, 1951.

UNITED NATIONS, *World Population Trends 1920–1947*, Population Studies No. 3, December, 1949.

——, *Economic Bulletin for Europe*, Vol. 1, No. 1, 1949.

——, *Demographic Yearbooks* 1949–50 and 1950–51.

——, Department of Social Affairs, *Population Bulletins*, No. 1, December, 1951; No. 2, 1952; also *Preliminary Report on World Social Situation*, New York, 1952.

——, *Measures for Economic Development of Underdeveloped Countries*, May, 1951.

——, *World Energy Supplies in Selected Years 1929–1950*, New York, September, 1952.

——, *Economic Survey of Europe since the War*, E.C.E., 1953.

VINER, J., *International Trade and Economic Development*, Oxford, Clarendon Press, 1953.

WALLACE, R., *A Dissertation on the Numbers of Mankind in Ancient and Modern Times*, Edinburgh, 1809 (1st Edition, 1753).

——, *Various Prospects of Mankind, Nature and Providence*, London, 1761

WIENER, NORBERT, *Cybernetics, or Control and Communication in the Animal and the Machine*, Cambridge, 1949.

——, *The Human Use of Human Beings*, London, 1950.

WILLCOX, WALTER F. (Ed.), *International Migration*, Vol. 1, *Statistics*, 1929; Vol. 2, *Interpretations*, 1931, International Labour Office, Bureau of Economic Research.

WOOLF, BARNET, "Environmental Effects in Quantitative Inheritance", p. 81 of *Quantitative Inheritance*, H.M.S.O., 1952, *q.v.*

WRIGHT, H., *Population*, Cambridge Economic Handbooks, V, 1923.

YEARBOOK OF THE WEST INDIES AND COUNTRIES OF THE CARIBBEAN, Skinner & Co., Ltd., London, 1951.

YULE, G. U. (C.B.E.), "The Growth of Population and the Factors which Control it", *Journal of the Royal Statistical Society*, Vol. LXXXVIII, 1925.

MADE AND PRINTED IN GREAT BRITAIN BY WILLIAM CLOWES AND SONS, LIMITED
LONDON AND BECCLES